Robert Munford

America's First Comic Dramatist

By

RODNEY M. BAINE

UNIVERSITY OF GEORGIA PRESS — ATHENS

For

JIMMY, WADE, AND ALICE

Contents

v

1980

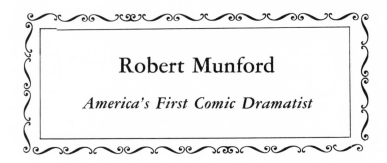

Robert Munford

America's First Comic Dramatist

Preface

A BIOGRAPHY of Robert Munford seems called for by his historical and intrinsic importance and by the still persisting lack of information about the man and his work. Despite the publication of his plays by his son, William, in 1798, historians of American drama and American literature have until recently been unacquainted with them. These were finally reprinted, *The Candidates* in 1948, edited by Mr. Jay B. Hubbell and Mr. Douglass Adair, and *The Patriots* in 1949, by Mr. Courtlandt Canby. *The Dictionary of American Biography* recognized his importance in a brief biography contributed by Mr. Armistead Gordon, Jr.; and in 1954 Mr. Hubbell devoted an excellent chapter to Munford in his *The South in American Literature*. These scholars have contributed to the revival of interest in a significant dramatist. But their biographical sketches and critical essays are inadequate to do justice to a writer of Munford's stature.

In supplementing the sparse and inaccurate information available about Munford, I have drawn especially upon Southside Virginia county records: familiarity with them has also helped to elucidate many aspects of the plays local in origin or significance. Search in libraries, moreover, has made available hitherto unrecorded correspondence, mostly military, which helps to throw light upon Munford's career. Search among Munford's descendants, however, has not yet revealed any letters which Munford himself received. Perhaps family tradition is here accurate: despite the fact that after Mrs. Munford died, William rented, then sold Richland, Munford's correspondence may have been abandoned there—to be consumed in the conflagration which destroyed the house.

For their assistance in the preparation of this study I am grateful to the following: Mr. Marcus A. McCorison, Librarian, American Antiquarian Society; Mr. John Alden, Keeper of Rare Books, Boston Public Library; Mr. Roger E. Stoddard, Curator, Harriss Collection, Brown University Library; Mr. Glenn B. Skillin, John Carter Brown Library; Mr. Douglass Adair, Cleremont Graduate

School; Mrs. Arline Custer, Acting Head, Manuscript Section, and Mr. Frederick R. Goff, Chief, Rare Book Division, Library of Congress; Mr. Jay B. Hubbell, Duke University, and Mrs. Virginia R. Gray, Assistant Curator, Duke University Library; Mr. Lester J. Cappon, Director, Institute of Early American History and Culture; Mr. John D. Kilbourne, Assistant to the Director, Maryland Historical Society; Mr. James J. Heslin, Director, New York Historical Society; Mr. Robert W. Hill, Keeper of Manuscripts, New York Public Library; Miss Katherine H. Laiblin, Librarian, Petersburg Public Library; Mr. Edwin Wolf, 2nd., Librarian, and Mr. Barney Chesnick, Curator, Library Company of Philadelphia; Mr. George C. Longest, Department of English, Richmond Professional Institute; Mr. Robert Rosenthal, Curator, Special Collections, University of Chicago Library; Mrs. Christine Burroughs, Interlibrary Loan Librarian, University of Georgia Library; Dr. Edward Gregory, the University of Richmond, and Miss Josephine Nunnally, Acting Librarian, University of Richmond Library; Mr. Richard Beale Davis, University of Tennessee; Mr. Kendon L. Stubbs, Assistant in Manuscripts, University of Virginia Library; Mr. Woodford B. Hackley, Secretary, Virginia Baptist Historical Society; Mr. Howson W. Cole, Curator of Manuscripts, Virginia Historical Society; Mr. William J. Van Schreeven, State Archivist, and Mr. Milton C. Russell, Head, Reference and Circulation Section, Virginia State Library; Mr. James A. Servies, Librarian, William and Mary Library; Mrs. Rose K. Belk, Librarian, Colonial Williamsburg; Mr. and Mrs. William Nash Beverley of Blandfield, Virginia; Mrs. Mary Haldane Coleman of Williamsburg; Mr. Wesley Alleyne De Laney of St. Louis; Mr. Nat G. Hutcheson, Clerk of Mecklenburg County; Mr. Robert H. Land of Alexandria; Mrs. Charles McCullough of New Bern, North Carolina; Mr. J. C. Sizemore, Deputy Clerk, Halifax County, Virginia; and Mrs. Sverre Tollefsen and Miss Page Williams of Richmond, both descendants of Munford.

For their reading the typescript, correcting numerous errors, and offering helpful advice, I am especially grateful to Mr. Herbert A. Elliott of South Hill, Virginia; to Mr. William B. Hill, Director of Prestwould House, Roanoke River Museum, Mecklenburg County; to my colleague Mr. Edd W. Parks, Alumni Foundation Distinguished Professor of English, the University of Georgia; and to my wife, Aline. However, as Dr. Johnson admitted in his final *Rambler* paper, I must apologize to them for the "obstinacy with which correction was rejected" on some points and "must remain accountable for all my faults." I am indebted also to the University

Center in Virginia and to the Southern Fellowship Fund for summer grants-in-aid which enabled me to undertake a biography of Munford and to the University of Georgia for research time and a travel grant which enabled me to complete it and to add the critical chapters. For his valuable assistance in checking proof and in compiling the Index, I am indebted to Mr. Robert Brummett.

For permission to quote hitherto unpublished material I wish to thank the following: Mr. James H. Renz, Assistant Librarian, The Earl Gregg Swem Library, The College of William and Mary in Virginia, for permission to quote from letters of William Munford; Mr. Edward Miles Riley, Director, Research Department, Colonial Williamsburg, for permission to quote from St. John Tucker's letter of 2 March 1781 to his wife; Mr. B. E. Powell, Librarian, Duke University Library—William Munford's "Robin Hood"; Mr. James J. Heslin, Director, the New York Historical Society— a letter from General Stevens to General Gates; Mr. Robert W. Hill, Keeper of Manuscripts, The New York Public Library—a letter from Munford to T. Bland; Mr. Howard H. Peckham, Director, The Clements Library, The University of Michigan— letters from Munford and Lewis Burwell to General Greene and an order from Greene to Burwell, from the Greene Papers; Mr. Howson B. Cole, Curator of Manuscripts, The Virginia Historical Society—letters from Munford to William Byrd III and from Matthew Phipps to Theoderick Munford; Mr. William J. Van Schreeven, State Archivist, The Virginia State Library—Legislative Petitions, Mecklenburg County, 14 May 1777; and Mr. and Mrs. William Nash Beverley of Blandfield—the Robert Beverley Letter Book deposited in the Library of Congress.

Except for expanding some conventional contractions in the correspondence of Munford, I have retained the spelling and punctuation of my sources.

RODNEY M. BAINE

English Department
University of Georgia

I

Student and Soldier

AFTER staging the first drama recorded in Colonial America, *The Bare and the Cubb*, and building at Williamsburg the first American playhouse, Virginia produced also America's first proper dramatic farce and first legitimate comedy. Both were written by Colonel Robert Munford of Mecklenburg County. He has never received proper recognition for his priorities. Colonel Thomas Forrest's *Disappointment*, produced in 1767, is not a true comedy, but a comic opera; and Royall Tyler's *Contrast*, at present regarded as America's first comedy, was written in 1787—several years after Munford's death. Munford's farce, *The Candidates*, was written perhaps as early as the winter of 1770-71; and his comedy, *The Patriots*, no later than 1783. Although these two plays were probably not produced during Munford's lifetime, they were obviously intended for production and may have been performed during the century. Theaters existed in several Virginia towns; even Mecklenburg County could boast its "playhouse," where the dramatist's son, William, once acted a part. But aside from being America's first farce and comedy, Munford's two plays deserve attention for themselves. Here are combined the felicitous artistry of a playwright familiar with the stagecraft of English comedy, and the keenly satirical wit of an imaginative observer playing upon the inequities and absurdities of the Virginia political and social scene. In its burlesque of Colonial elections *The Candidates* is still amusing; and *The Patriots* poses what were then and what remain today questions of vital importance—the questions of loyalty, of allegiance, and of the persecution of minority groups.

Through his parents Robert Munford of Mecklenburg County was allied with many prominent Virginia families. The connections of his mother, Anna Bland Munford, were particularly distinguished. One of her brothers, Richard Bland, represented Virginia in the First Continental Congress and was, in the judgment of Thomas Jefferson, "the most learned and logical man of those who

1

took prominent lead in public affairs."[1] Her other brother, Theoderick, was also outstanding. One of her sisters, Mary Bland, married Colonel Henry Lee of Lee's Hall; the other, Elizabeth, married William Beverley of Blandfield, son of Robert Beverley the historian and Ursula Byrd. By her mother, Elizabeth Randolph Bland, daughter of Colonel William Randolph of Turkey Island, the dramatist's mother was related to the Randolphs and thus to many other eminent families of Virginia.

From the early eighteenth century the Munfords too were a family of some prominence. But the brilliance with which that family then emerged in both politics and literature and which it has continued to exhibit in those fields has induced some of its descendants and admirers to seek for a more romantic beginning than they can substantiate. In his *Random Recollections*, for example, Beverley Bland Munford pointed to a Thomas Munford, spelled "Mountford" in Smith's lists, who was with Captain John Smith in the *First Supply*, took part in an exploration of the Chesapeake, and was co-author of the account of the expedition published by Smith in his *Historie of Virginia*. But this Thomas Munford soon returned to England, and no evidence has shown him or his descendants again in Virginia.[2] An even more romantic lineage was suggested by the Reverend Philip Slaughter: "There is a tradition that the name was originally De Montford, and that the blood was that of the family of the Earl of Leicester—the Virginia representative having been proscribed for political offenses, and forced to fly the kingdom. To the support of this tradition it may be stated, that in one of the grants to Ro. Munford the name is spelled *Mountfort*."[3] Slender evidence indeed, if so it can be called.

The lineage which Munford would doubtless have selected for himself is unfortunately out of the question. He could not have been the direct descendant of the brilliant Restoration actor and playwright William Mountfort, who in his youth spelled his name "Munford," and his equally gifted wife Susanna Peircivall (later, Verbruggen): both their children were daughters. But Munford might have descended from a collateral branch of that numerous Staffordshire family.[4]

All that can be demonstrated with any assurance is that Robert Munford the dramatist's grandfather was evidently the son of James Munford, to whom were granted 20 April 1689 the same 50¼ acres in Westover Parish which in 1704 Robert Munford I patented. James Munford's wife seems to have been the daughter of Robert Wyatt.[5] It is possible that the great-grandfather James was the son of James Mountfort, Sr., of Charles City County, who died in or shortly after 1655, leaving a son, James, then twelve years old.[6]

Comparatively undistinguished during the seventeenth century, the Munfords were from the early eighteenth century a family of some position. Robert Munford I, grandfather of the dramatist, began his rise to prominence shortly after December of 1701, when he married Martha Kennon, daughter of Colonel Richard Kennon of Conjurer's Neck.[7] In 1704 he began to accumulate considerable holdings in land. In 1720 he acquired what was evidently one of the first Virginia grants on the Roanoke River; and by 1728 he held well over 15,000 acres in Prince George, Surry, and Brunswick counties. For several years he acted as overseer for William Byrd II on his Appomattox plantation, a few miles from Westover. From at least 1706 until 1717 he was Byrd's attorney; and he seems at times to have managed Byrd's legal affairs, sometimes acting by deputy.[8] In frequent overnight visits to Westover, Munford combined business with pleasure. He and Byrd often shot wild pigeons with bow and arrow; and they spent considerable time at cricket and billiards, where the guest was careful never to win more than two bits.[9]

Munford was not only an agreeable and convivial guest; he was a considerate host. When in 1728 Byrd ran his Dividing Line near Munford's Roanoke plantations, Munford recommended most of the men who accompanied Byrd on the expedition and arranged for refreshment for the hungry surveyors along the way, providing a young steer at each stop on or near his plantations. When in 1733 Byrd undertook his journey to the "Land of Eden," the ailing Munford sent along his eldest son, James, and again arranged to make Byrd's trip as pleasant as he could. On his return Byrd commented, "An honester a man, a fairer trader, or a kinder friend, this country never produced: God send any of his sons may have the grace to take after him."[10]

Byrd found the inhabitants of Southside Virginia "mine-mad." On his trip he evidently passed through lands on Butcher's Creek which, thirty odd years later, Robert Munford the dramatist was to acquire and make his principal plantation: "through the woods to Butcher's Creek, which hath its name from an honest fellow that lives upon it. This place is about six miles from Colonel Stith's works and can also boast of a very fair show of copper ore. It is dug out of the side of a hill that rises gradually from the creek to the house. The good man was from home himself, but his wife, who was as old as one of the Sibyls, refreshed us with

an ocean of milk."[11] On their return Byrd and his party found their
host at home: "Mr. Butcher received us kindly and we had a
true Roanoke entertainment of pork upon pork, and pork again
upon that. He told us he had been one of the first seated in
that remote part of the country and in the beginning had been
forced, like the great Nebuchadnezzar, to live a considerable time
upon grass. This honest man set a mighty value on the mine he
fancied he had in his pasture and showed us some of the ore, which
he was made to believe was a gray copper and would certainly
make his fortune. But there's a bad distemper rages in those parts
that grows very epidemical. The people are all mine-mad and,
neglecting to make corn, starve their families in hopes to live in
great plenty hereafter."[12]

The political rise of Robert Munford I can be unquestionably
attributed largely to the influence of William Byrd. In May, 1709
Byrd secured from the President of the Council of Virginia a
commission appointing Munford Clerk of the Court of Prince
George County, but when Munford refused to halve the fees with
the incumbent, he was rejected by the Court.[13] Some time before
10 May 1715, however, he had become a Justice of Prince George
County; and by 8 January 1716, a Major in the Prince George
militia. By 8 June 1729 he had risen to the rank of Colonel. Before
1720 he had evidently been for some time a vestryman of Bristol
Parish, for on 23 November 1721 he was elected churchwarden
for the South Side of Bristol Parish, and he was regularly re-
elected during the decade.[14] In 1720 and again in 1722 he was
elected by his county to the House of Burgesses. He attended his
last vestry meeting in June, 1734 and died evidently by March of
the following year, when he was replaced on the vestry by his
second son, Robert.[15]

Robert Munford II also inherited from his father wide property
and political prestige, and the friendship of William Byrd II.
He was doubtless assisted in his rise to prominence also by an
advantageous marriage, presumably in the early 1730's, to Anna
Bland. As early as 1733 Robert Munford II was helping to make
Byrd's trip comfortable along the Roanoke plantations; and like
his father, he frequently made overnight visits to Westover,
whence he departed in the mornings, according to Byrd, "the best
with a dram of cherry brandy in his belly."[16] By 15 November
1736 he had become a captain in the militia of Prince George
County.[17] During the Assembly of 1736-1740 he represented his
county in the House of Burgesses. Evidently his familiarity with
Indian conditions prompted his appointment in 1740 as envoy to

assure peace with the Catawbas and Cherokees. Returning in June of 1741, he brought a belt of wampum from the Catawbas and a peace pipe from the Cherokees as tokens of their acceptance of peace, but reported "that while he was among the Cheraukees a Party of the Northern Indians had fallen upon some of the Cheraukees and killed or taken & carried away about Sixty of them; And that the Cheraukees had thereupon entertained a Suspicion of him, as if he had brought those Indians upon them, and while he was amusing them with Pease was only contriving the more easily to destroy them; And that he was in danger of being killed by them. . . ."[18] Meanwhile Munford suffered such serious financial reverses that during the winter of 1739-1740 he was forced to mortgage his mansion, Whitehall. Unfortunate in litigation, harassed by monetary worries, and presumably ailing in health, he took to drink. On 11 May 1743 William Beverley complained that most of the estate was being sold to pay the drunken husband's debts.[19] Early in 1745, Beverley was writing to aid his widowed sister-in-law, doubtless spurred by his wife, who was indignant at her "grate relations" for their failure to pay off the debt:[20]

It is now some months since my Wife's Sister Mrs. Anna Munford has been left a poor distressed widow with two Sons and a daughter in very mean circumstances (I have taken Robert her Eldest son & Mr. Lee her daughter Elizabeth) the house & 800 Acres of Land where she lives being Mortgaged to one Mr. Theophilus ffield for about £360 Sterling and no hopes of Redeeming it, without your kind Assistance for neither her Brothers nor my Self have any Ready money to assist her, and before her Eldest Son Comes of Age the Interest will eat it out . . . tho' her husband was a Sot & used her very Ill on all Occasions, yet she always behaved herself toward him on all accounts as a good & dutiful wife ought to do. . . .[21]

Robert Munford III, the dramatist, was born about 1737.[22] During the eight years which preceded his father's death, leisurely plantation life must have been pleasant to the boy. Whitehall was not in the grand style of Tidewater Colonial architecture of the eighteenth century: it had only two rooms below and two above, with a ten foot passageway. There were, however, another similar house and numerous outbuildings: a separate kitchen, a dairy with a stone floor, a meat and smokehouse, a barn, a tobacco house, two stables, a coach house, and several additional storehouses and warehouses.[23] Young Robert must have known early all the processes of growing, curing, and shipping tobacco, the staple crop; and he must have known well also the orchards down by the Appomattox River. Here at Whitehall, his sister Elizabeth, his elder by several years, must have frequently been detailed to look after him, as well as his younger brother, Theoderick, born in 1742.[24] Only six miles down the Appomattox lived several cousins, children of his uncle James Munford and Elizabeth Bolling Munford; and also near was his cousin Theoderick Bland, Jr.

After the death of his father in 1745, Robert was, as has been seen, taken by his uncle Beverley to Blandfield. Perhaps it was just as well that he was away from home during the rather perplexed courtship which followed. George Currie, an enterprizing Scot, evidently undertook to manage for Mrs. Munford the Roanoke estate; in June, 1747, he registered in Lunenburg County her power of attorney. In September she instituted suit against him. Then, suddenly, before November of the same year, they were married.[25]

But if life, once leisurely, had become puzzling at Whitehall, it was spacious and serene at Blandfield. The Beverley estate covered several square miles and extended three miles along the Rappahannock; and the spacious Blandfield made Whitehall seem cramped. Here in Essex County young Munford evidently spent his boyhood, from the age of eight until he was about fourteen, riding about with his cousins, duck-shooting in the marshes surrounding the little island just offshore, and swimming at the sand bar off one of the creeks which empty into the Rappahannock, for the rest of the shore is quite muddy. Not all time was play time; he studied his lessons with his cousins and read in his uncle's excellent library.

When the boys had learned all they could from local masters and time for more formal schooling arrived, Mr. Beverley made arrangements to take them to England, as was the custom of Virginia planters who could afford to send their sons abroad. On 2 July 1750 Munford embarked for England with his uncle Beverley, Mrs. Beverley, Robert and Anna Beverley, and William Henry Fairfax.[26] By 7 August the party docked at Liverpool; and on 13 August the boys attended a play—perhaps the future dramatist's first taste of the theater. Then, leaving the family behind in Liverpool, Mr. Beverley looked about for a proper school and finally settled upon Beverley School, where with the help of the master, John Clarke, he was able to secure comfortable accommodations. Hither he returned on 14 September with his party, and here at Beverley School, after the treat of another play, he placed the three boys.

Munford was fortunate in his uncle's choice. Clarke was an able master; and his classical scholarship had been praised by Richard Bentley, England's greatest classical scholar. Moreover life at Beverley must have been a happy one for young Munford. School must not have been particularly difficult after the able training his uncle had provided in Virginia, and living with the Beverleys must have been pleasant. His uncle treated him as a member of the family and allowed him as much pocket money as he gave his own son. He furnished the boys with necessities at school, with pen-knives and even "ponies" for their Aesop's *Fables*. With an eye on their social graces as well as their intellectual development he arranged, too, for them to attend Mr. Wharton's dancing school.

After about a year the party transferred from Beverley School to Wakefield. When in April of 1751 John Clarke succeeded the Reverend Benjamin Wilson as Headmaster of Wakefield and agreed to defray part of the expenses of their removal, the Beverleys decided to accompany him. They set off for Wakefield on 2 May 1751, and upon their arrival Mr. Beverley immediately arranged for the boys to attend Mr. Graves' dancing school as well as Wakefield School. Here at Wakefield Munford received a thorough classical education under competent masters. Founded in Queen Elizabeth's reign, Wakefield Grammar School was one of the best preparatory schools in England. If the original rules were still enforced, a rigorous schedule kept the students busy from six in the morning until six in the evenings, or in winter from sunrise until sunset.[27] Clarke's usher, Henry Wilson, who accompanied him from Beverley, supervised the boys in the lower forms. Although Munford never acquired an education to match that of his father's friend William Byrd of Westover, the love of learning inculcated by John Clarke and Henry Wilson remained with the dramatist throughout his life; and during his last years he was engaged in translating Ovid's *Metamorphoses*, one of the first books which he studied at Wakefield.[28] Here at Wakefield he must have read some classical drama. The first author recommended by the foundation charter for study was Terence, and when Clarke arrived he must have added to the list of texts his favorite, Aristophanes. Possibly Clarke encouraged the boys in private theatricals; and abetted by his uncle, Munford must have had opportunities of seeing performances by players of the Yorkshire dramatic circuit.

Wakefield was a favorite school for Virginians: half a dozen were there when Munford arrived, including Richard Henry Lee and an unidentified brother; and hither within a few years came cousin Theoderick Bland, Jr., and Robert Bolling, who arrived 24 September 1751, only a few months after the Beverleys. Writing several years later, Bolling described ironically his progress in languages: "God only knows how many classes he passed in the

course of two years. He was then put in the same class in which
were young Beverley, Fairfax and Munford, and about the same
time began to learn French; of that language he was particularly
fond, and soon acquired it under Monsieur DeBournai, (or as he
was then called Monsieur des Bureaux) and afterwards under
Monsieur des Granges, so that he understood it better than the
Latin, notwithstanding the great progress he had made in that
language."[29]

When his Uncle Beverley died, on 28 February 1756, leaving
in his will no provision for his nephew,[30] Munford returned to
Virginia. Upon his arrival he must have gone immediately to visit
his mother in Prince George County. Here he saw, possibly
for the first time, his half-sisters, Anne and Margaret, and got over
the awkward meeting with his stepfather, George Currie.

Since his stepson's departure for England, Currie had been quite
active. At the formation of Halifax County, in May, 1752, Currie
had become the county clerk. He was also a tireless surveyor,
developer, and speculator, both near Petersburg and to the west:
in Halifax County he surveyed, located, and built the first court
house, prison, stocks, and pillory, subsequently acted as jailer, and
owned the ordinary at the county seat. When in 1755 the county
seat was moved, he again built the court house, stocks, and prison;
and during that year and the next he acquired over 5700 acres
of land in the county. In 1753 his aspiration to become a burgess
was nullified: although he was clerk of Halifax County, evidently
he could not qualify as burgess because he could not satisfy the
requirement of three years of residence in the county.[31]

With the advice of his mother, his stepfather, and his uncle
Theoderick, Munford arranged to study law at Williamsburg in
the office of his second cousin, King's Attorney Peyton Randolph.
Munford went to Williamsburg to make the arrangements and on
23 August 1756 reported to his uncle, sending his love to his aunt
and cousins:

The Attorney has wrote an Answer to your Letter by Ned,
which I hope will be satisfactory. I'm very sorry my Horse should
occasion any Disturbance. Mr. Currie when I saw him last was saying
he had not a Horse that would carry him to Hallifax. I told him
I expected Jeter would call for mine, but was unwilling that should
be an Impediment to my obliging him, therefore was willing he
should have him. I was entirely to blame for not mentioning it
to you, which I wou'd have done, had I thought of it. Mr. Currie
will send you the Horse on his return, when I shall be much
oblig'd to you for your care of him. He is entirely at your's, or

any of your Family's Service. Mr. Banister has the News of Consequence. I wrote you in a former Letter my reception from the Attorney. He has mention'd no Terms to me as yet, but hope they will be such as a Gentleman may live on.[32]

Arrangements for Munford's legal training were evidently completed in the fashion usual at that time: he read law under the guidance of and doubtless acted as secretary and assistant for Randolph, a brilliant, but perhaps somewhat indolent man; at least Randolph was not aggressive in seeking business. Probably Munford lived at Randolph's home, in the middle of town, only a block from the Governor's Palace, just as Thomas Jefferson was to live with George Wythe six years later when he began the study of law at the same age and in a similar fashion. Here in Williamsburg Munford could hear all the cases brought before the General Court, could read law in Randolph's library or in the law library at the Capitol, and could attend plays. He apparently kept his servant, Ned, but did not, like Jefferson, keep his horse, avoiding the temptation, perhaps, of frequent visits to his mother and uncle in Prince George County. He evidently settled down to business with serious determination, resolved also to keep an eye on his younger brother Theoderick, who was, at the age of fourteen still probably a student at William and Mary.[33]

Munford arrived too late to join in the excitement of 2 May 1756, when a group of 150 lawyers and other volunteers from Williamsburg, under the leadership of Peyton Randolph, volunteered to provide their own mounts and proceed to the assistance of George Washington.[34] Probably Munford would even then have accompanied his mentor. When the opportunity actually arrived, Munford doubtless had the encouragement of Randolph and of one of the Governor's Council, William Byrd III. Soon after the French and Indian War broke out, Munford became an officer in the newly formed Second Virginia Regiment and took part in the capture of Fort Duquesne. During the early summer of 1758 he quickly raised a company for the new regiment commanded by Byrd; and a letter of 19 June 1758 from Governor General Francis Fauquier to Byrd, dispatched by Munford himself, authorized his commission, if he excelled in recruiting, as the ranking lieutenant, or "captain-lieutenant," in charge of one of the companies nominally commanded by one of the field officers.[35] He evidently captained Byrd's own company. On the sixth of July, marching with Byrd from Winchester with eight companies, Munford reached camp near Fort Cumberland, where as senior officer Colonel George Washington, of the First Virginia Regiment, took precedence over the young Byrd. From this camp Munford wrote to his uncle Theoderick Bland two vivid letters describing the early stages of the campaign:

Camp, near Fort Cumberland, July 6th, 1758.

HON'D SIR,

Had opportunities offered, as frequently as inclination wou'd have induced me to write to you, you might have read a letter from me every encampment. After being delay'd at Winchester, five or six weeks longer than expected, (in which time, I was ordered express to Williamsburg, and allowed but a day after my return to prepare,) we push'd off into the wide ocean. I was permitted to walk every step of the way to this humble fort, to eat little, and lay hard, over mountain, thro' mud and water, yet as merry and hearty as ever. Our flankers and sentrys pretend they saw the enemy daily, but they never approached us. A detachment is this moment ordered off, to clear a road thirty miles, and our companies to cover the working party. We are in fine scalping ground, I assure you; the guns pop about us, and you may see the fellows prick up their ears like deer every moment. Our Col. is an example of fortitude in either danger or hardships, and by his easy, polite behaviour, has gain'd not only the regard but affection of both officers and soldiers. He has kindly invited me to his table for the campaign, offer'd me any sum of money I may have occasion for, without charging either principal or interest, and signified his approbation of my conduct hitherto in such a manner as is to me of advantage. In passing my recruiting account, I was allowed 18 [shillings] per man, you may judge how much I was loser, when several officers had 40 *s.* * * * * * * * * * *

Col. Charles Carter Junr. had a horse of mine in keeping till my return, where he may remain if you think proper. The ball money and forage money allow'd me amounts to £66. In every thing possible I shall be upon the frugal scheme. You may depend upon hearing by all opportunities from, dear Dr., your truly affect, and ever

Obliged nephew, &c.

To MRS. BLAND.

HONR'D MADAM,

Tho' I've hardly a moment at my own disposal, I can't omit sending a few words to my dear aunt. Employed from sun to sun, yet from light to night, am I mindful of my dear distant friends. That you and yours may enjoy every blessing that Heaven can bestow, is the tribute of a heart sincerely yours, &c.

P. S. My love to the lasses.[36]

A few months later Munford, like his superior officers, was chafing at delay and was protesting indignantly because General

Forbes favored the new Pennsylvania road for the approach to Fort Duquesne. Writing again to his Uncle Theoderick Bland, he complained:

Camp, near Fort Cumberland, August 4th, 1758.

HON'D SIR,

If 'tis honorable to be in the service of one's country, 'tis a reputation gain'd by the most cruel hardships you can imagine, occasioned more by a real anxiety for its welfare, than by what the poor carcase suffers. Every officer seems discontented in camp, happy on command, so deep is the interest of our country implanted in the minds of all. Sometimes the army wears a gloomy, then a joyous aspect, just as the news either confirms our stay here, or immediate departure. The Genl., with the small-pox in one, the flux in the other division of our forces, and no provision ready, are indeed excuses for our being here at present; yet all might have been prevented. A few hearty prayers are every moment offered up for those self-interested Pennsylvanians who endeavour to prevail on our Genl. to cut a road for their convenience, from Ray's Town to Fort Du-Quesne. That a trifling good to particulars, shoud retard what wou'd conduce to the general welfare! 'Tis a set of dirty Dutchmen, they say, that keep us here! It would be impertinent to condemn, yet I must [think] our leaders too deliberate at this important juncture, when all are warm for action, all breathing revenge against an enemy that have even dared to scalp our men before our eyes. The amusement we have in the mean time is only following the brave dogs over the mountains for some miles, and our sole satisfaction sufficient fatigue to make us sleep sound. An old scoundrel has intimated to the Genl. that the Virginians have bribed the guides, for that 'tis practicable to go the new road, contrary to their report. We have lost all our Indians by the assistance of a man, the [afore said] old dog, who interposed thro' some dirty views he has of superseding Mr. Atkin.[37] Thus are our officers in a manner ruin'd by persons whose souls scorn a thought that tends not immediately to their own advantage. I'm sorry to live upon my country when I've so small a prospect of repaying her by any service. We shall march to Ray's Town shortly, thence to the Fort, if permitted. I shall embrace the next opportunity of writing you our transactions, and am as always, dear sir, your most

Aff'te nephew, &c.

P. S. By express, we have an acc't that some of the enemy Indians have joined the Pennsylvanians.

TO MRS. BLAND.

HONR'D MADM,

I am well and lousie, but still your affect'e nephew, &c.[38]

According to Washington, Byrd's regiment, which included a large number of gentleman farmers, was not a particularly able combat unit. Moreover smallpox broke out at Raystown, and the regiment lacked a surgeon. A great many were ill of the flux, as indeed was Byrd himself; and those who were not sick rapidly became "low Spirited and dejected," despite the fact that wagon trains for the Virginia regiments sometimes brought more rum than powder. For these vexations, privations, and sicknesses there were few consolations. One was the presence of an able, seasoned senior colonel, Washington; another was the companionship of a congenial junior colonel, Byrd, and of other neighbors among the officers. Possibly, to quicken interest, Munford helped to organize among the soldiers such a group of players as had performed for Washington at Fort Cumberland in January of the previous year.[39] But probably unknown to Munford was Thomas Godfrey, who took part in the campaign as an ensign of the Pennsylvania militia and who may have had in his pocket a draft of America's first tragedy, *The Prince of Parthia*.

Except for skirmishing, Munford probably saw little fighting on this campaign: the Second Virginia Regiment was involved in no major combat on the march to Fort Duquesne, and it was abandoned about the time Forbes reached it. After the Second Virginia Regiment was disbanded, Munford evidently returned to Williamsburg, in early 1759, to resume his legal studies there. He took no part in the attempt during the autumn of 1760 to raise the siege of Fort Loudon.[40]

When Peyton Randolph was satisfied with his knowledge of law, Munford moved to Lunenburg County to take possession of the land and slaves which his father had willed him there on the banks and the islands of the Roanoke River. From 1760 Munford was a gentleman planter of Southside Virginia.

II

Southside Planter

THE southern section of Lunenburg County, soon to become
Mecklenburg County, where Munford made his home from 1760
until his death, presents an undulating landscape of hills and valleys
cut into unequal sections by the Roanoke River.[1] Unlike the James
and the Appomattox and the York, the Roanoke was not an important avenue of transportation. Only in the following century
was the river sufficiently cleared so that boats carrying nine or
ten hogsheads of tobacco could traverse its shallows. Normally
it was fairly placid, but in flood times rushing torrents swept
away trees, crops, animals, barns, and houses. Along the river
a system of ferries was maintained. Munford's step-father, George
Currie, had by 1748 established a ferry at Munford's Quarter.[2]
Denied transportation by water, the inhabitants were forced to
rely upon a network of rough roads. The survey, construction,
and maintenance of roads and bridges were the first concern
of county officials; and every gentleman had his part in their
superintendence and maintenance. Munford himself had his roads
to oversee and to keep in repair.

The land was well forested with oak, pine, and hickory, but
by the early eighteenth century little game was left in the region.
From the southwest, however, a brisk trade in skins continued; and
ordinarily Munford's brother, Theoderick, who as early as 1763
had his own ship, the *Hawk*, carried several hogsheads of skins as
part of his cargo.[3]

The money crop was tobacco, and since specie was rare, tobacco
formed a legal medium of exchange. Each year the crop was
harvested and sent to warehouses along the Appomattox. On
the plantations were grown also corn, wheat, sugar cane, and all
the other staple crops needed for the planter's family and his
hands. At that time Virginia even produced wheat for export:
Captain Munford's cargo normally included about two hundred
barrels.

13

By 1760 Lunenburg County was fairly well "civilized." There were no towns of any importance, but the population had grown rapidly, and claims for wolf bounties had become rare. In 1733, when Byrd traversed it, it had been only sparsely populated, and to Byrd the few settlers had seemed coarse and lazy. But since that time these shiftless vagrants and irresponsible tenants had been largely replaced by numerous small landowners and a fairly sizeable group of slaveholders. There were in residence no large land proprietors, like Beverley or Byrd, and Southside Virginia could not match the elegant brick mansions of Tidewater Virginia. Instead, planters built neat frame homes, and painted them white.

For schooling there was little opportunity except that offered by the parson at the school sometimes held at the glebe or by a tutor living with a prominent family like the Marrables, the Deloneys, or the Skipwiths.[4] Some parents taught their own children: family tradition records that Captain James Speed taught his children not only English composition, but Latin and Greek as well.[5] Mecklenburg County records of 1769 mention the "burnt Schoolhous,"[6] presumably where the Reverend John Pugh taught. His successor, the Reverend John Cameron, an able classical scholar educated at King's College, Aberdeen, was so competent a master that Munford sent his son, William, to him, both when Cameron was endeavoring to hold his school in Mecklenburg and later when he moved to Petersburg.[7]

In 1765 most of the inhabitants of Mecklenburg County conformed to the Established, Anglican Church. As early as 6 November 1734 the Vestry of St. Andrews Parish had instructed William Toms to minister to those remote districts; on alternate Sundays he was to read services at John Butcher's and Joseph Colson's, five miles up the river on Munford's Quarter.[8] The dissenters, however, made increasing inroads. Even before Munford moved into Southside Virginia, in 1758 a Baptist congregation had been established at Bluestone;[9] and on 8 April 1765 the Mecklenburg Court authorized the construction of two new meeting houses; at one services were evidently conducted by Dennis Larke.[10] By 1770 the Baptists had become well established, and during the year two well-known Baptist ministers began their work in Mecklenburg County. Elijah Baker was pastor briefly at Malone's Church; and John Williams, former sheriff of Lunenburg County, began his ministry at a church on Allen's Creek, near Munford's Richland.[11]

But neither the dissenters nor the Anglicans were completely happy in Mecklenburg County. In February, 1772 the Baptists of Mecklenburg, like those in several other Southside counties, petitioned the House of Burgesses that they found themselves "restricted in the Exercise of their Religion, their Teachers imprisoned under various Pretences, and the Benefits of the Toleration Act denied them."[12] As senior magistrate of Mecklenburg County, Munford was perhaps the particular traget of this petition. Though he did not bother the Methodists in their places of worship, he was evidently inclined to be rather severe on outdoor preaching, and he swore the peace against John Williams, who had to come into court, on 14 July 1772, and give security.[13] Perhaps this incident led Williams subsequently to his concerted, organized efforts on behalf of religious freedom.

Anglicans too were unhappy in Mecklenburg. As early as 21 March 1772 some of the parishioners of St. James were petitioning the House of Burgesses that the parish vestry be dissolved; and on 9 May 1774 they reiterated their plea:

. . . the Vestry of the said Parish, having caused three large Churches and a Chapel to be built, consulted as to the Situations thereof, the Conveniency of the Vestrymen themselves, rather than that of the Petitioners; and that the said Vestry having agreed to receive into the Parish a Minister, who was approved of by the Parishioners, afterwards suddenly received another Minister, who was a Stranger to them; and that the said Vestry, in Order to enable one *Rogers*, a notorious Gamester, of infamous Character, to obtain holy Orders, gave him a Recommendation to a Benefice, but took a Bond from him, with Security, in the Penalty of one thousand Pounds, that he should not claim under that Title; and therefore praying that the said Vestry may be dissolved.[14]

Evidently Munford persuaded the Committee on Religion that the petition was not urgent; at any rate, after he was placed on the committee, consideration of the petition was delayed until the following session. But this rebuff did not faze the petitioners: on 17 May 1774 they asked for a partition of the parish; and on 26 May they hit again at the vestry, asserting "that *William Hunt*, one of the Vestrymen of the said Parish hath lately been detected in a Villanous Action; and therefore praying that the Vestry of the said Parish may be dissolved."[15]

Perhaps Munford gradually became more tolerant on religious matters, but the evidence is conflicting. On 29 May 1777 he was not among the signers of the Mecklenburg petition on behalf of the Established Church; and on 15 October 1779 he was on the Committee on Religion which brought in the bill to abolish levies and thus accomplish the separation of church and state.[16] Yet on 3 December 1779 he voted against relieving dissenters from paying double taxes.[17] His tolerance must have been either broadened or exacerbated when that same year the Reverend Archibald McRobert, who had married his sister, Elizabeth, withdrew from the Establishment to become an Independent and subsequently a Presbyterian.[18]

On week days Mecklenburgers found a number of diversions. Their relaxations included ninepins, gaming, cockfighting, drinking, and politics. A favorite was horseracing. The quarter mile became a Southside specialty soon after Munford made his home there. While he was studying law in Williamsburg a number of his Tidewater friends and relatives had been horse fanciers. William Byrd III especially had, like his father, imported quite a string of horses and mares.[19] Later, in the 1770's racing became the rage in Mecklenburg County. At this time owners of thoroughbreds included not only Lewis and Thacker Burwell, but Jacob Bugg, Edward Davis, Henry Deloney, Thomas Feild, John Goode, Sr., William Lucas, Solomon Patillo, Francis Ruffin, Sir Peyton Skipwith, James Speed, Sr., Colonel George Tarry, and D. Williams.[20] Some of them, especially Colonel Tarry, a particular friend who lived just across the Roanoke, and John Goode, Sr., had quite a string. On 23 September 1782 Sir Peyton advertised eighty blooded mares to be sold 15 December, "the day after the great race to be run by Mr. Goode and others."[21]

In their mores and morals the inhabitants of Lunenburg and Mecklenburg counties seem to have been no different from those of the other Southern counties on the fringe of the tobacco belt. Murder was a rare sensation, as was mayhem, but in 1776 Philip Watson bit a chunk from the ear of John Hudson.[22] There was a horse stealing on the average of every five years, and twice in a score of years Mecklenburgers were tried for hog-stealing. Moral lapses were viewed sometimes sternly, sometimes leniently, depending perhaps upon who happened to be foreman of the Grand Jury. After the Great Awakening and during the Revolution, neighbors were sometimes inclined to be rather severe, and the Grand Juries frequently returned numerous sinners whose lapses had not a whit disturbed the gentlemen justices, who were evidently inclined to view these pecadilloes askance and dismiss the charges without a hearing. Among the offenses for which many were annually called to account were failure to keep the roads in repair, selling liquor without a license, swearing (even in one's own home!), unlawful gambling, and drunkenness. Patent sexual immorality was censured: those who lived in fornication, or "a Dultery," as the clerk customarily recorded it, were ordinarily fined and released; and begetting or bearing a bastard occasioned a special assessment. The father either contributed to the upkeep of his bastard or went to jail. Sometimes the laws were administered with a Puritanical severity. For example, in May of 1761 John Dunn was cited for "Profane Swearing" and failing to attend divine services.[23] Sunday was to be kept holy: on 8 May 1769 Sir Peyton Skipwith was fined for "Suffering his slaves driving the wagon, And Roleing Tobacco on the Sabbath day."[24] In this section of Southside Virginia Munford arrived in 1760 and assumed the responsibilities of a Virginia gentleman planter.

During this year, moreover, or early in 1761 Munford married his cousin and childhood playmate Anna Beverley, probably before her brother Robert returned from England. Two daughters were soon born to them: Elizabeth Bevereley, on 28 March 1762, and Ursula Anna, probably the next year.[25]

Doubtless aided by the dowry of £1500 and land left Anna by her father,[26] Munford at once began to enlarge and improve his plantations, so that by 1765 he had become one of the most prominent landholders and slaveowners in the county.[27] To the Finneywood and Occaneachy plantations in Lunenburg County, willed him by his father, Munford began steadily to add. On 29 May 1760 he secured, for £5/15, a grant of 1150 acres on the branches of Blue Stone Creek,[28] and during the following year he acquired additional property there from his neighbor Matthew Marrable, one of the justices of Lunenburg County and a burgess, subsequently for many years Munford's colleague representing Mecklenburg County with him in the House of Burgesses.[29] Soon, however, Munford began to concentrate his holdings at the mouth of Butcher's Creek, which empties south into the Roanoke River. Before 18 October 1766, with the assistance of his overseer Drury Smith, he cleared a fishing place on the Roanoke; and a few years later he purchased for £200 a fishing place at the point of Cow Island.[30] In May of 1779 he reopened the Occaneachy Ferry which his stepfather had established on the Roanoke in 1748.[31]

Upon his plantations Munford naturally grew tobacco. Upon it depended the credit and luxuries of the Virginia planter. Unfortunately Munford, like Washington, began at an unlucky time, when prices for the last, 1759 crop had sunk to a very low level and when a series of misfortunes made the years 1760 and 1761 equally disastrous for tobacco growers. He raised in addition the staple crops needed to supply his plantation with necessities: his corn he ground at his own water grist mill; he built up large herds of cattle for his milk and butter, and more than enough to slaughter for meat. His growing herds of sheep provided wool for warm clothes and blankets and occasionally mutton for the table.[32] Like all other Southerners he had large herds of hogs to furnish pork for the tables of his slaves.

The plantations were cultivated by an increasing number of slaves. Survivors from the six negroes that he had been willed in 1743, with their increase, were obviously an inadequate force for farming on a large scale.[33] Munford must have purchased additional slaves before or soon after his marriage, for by 1764, only four years after he settled down in Southside Virginia, he had thirty-four tithables working under his overseer Drury Smith alone.[34] This number steadily increased until in 1782 he had on his plantation, in addition to five whites, ninety-one slaves; and at his death these numbered one hundred and five.[35] His slaves he dressed in cotton jackets and breeches, Osnaburg shirts, and leather gambadoes. He evidently treated them more humanely than most owners did. Although he accepted unquestioningly the system of slavery, his poems suggest a sympathetic understanding of their servitude;[36] and after his death Mrs. Munford impoverished the family by keeping too many of her devoted servants. Occasionally, however, a slave ran away. On 16 May 1771, for example, Cuffy was advertised—a large negro about forty years old, six feet, two inches tall, and poxed.[37] Cuffy was discovered in Elizabeth City County, whither he had gone to visit friends.[38] Cuthie, a negro woman who ran away in December of 1778, was fleeing not from Munford, but the Reverend John Cameron, to whom she had evidently been loaned some time earlier.[39] More trouble was created by Jack, a low, squat fellow with bow legs and bloodshot eyes, who ran away in 1766. Already he had been branded on the cheeks with Munford's initials for his principal part in "promoting the late disorderly meetings among the Negroes," and he was fleeing to escape prosecution for the robberies he had committed. He came to a bad end. In 1772 he raped a white woman, a neighbor of Munford, and was executed.[40]

Only in 1765 did Munford decide upon and purchase a site for his new mansion. "The location," wrote a later owner of Richland Hill, "provides an explanation for the later history of the place. To the east of Butcher's Creek is a plateau containing some thirty acres or more, sloping sharply to the creek on the west, to the river lowlands on the south and a branch to the east. On the

north is a more gentle decline. It was an ideal location for a plantation residence."[41] Like practically all other Southside mansions (Sir
Peyton Skipwith's stone Prestwould was built after Munford's
death), Munford's Richland was constructed of timber, shingled,
and painted white. Unpretentious, but spacious, it was a two-story,
hiproofed building with one-story wings.[42] From the entrance porch,
the front door opened upon a commodious hallway, with drawing
room and dining room on either hand. Twelve could be seated at
table there, and with the eight Windsor chairs from the hall, room
could be made in the drawing room and hall for two additional
tables. There were ample China dishes, butter pots, pewter plates,
teacups and saucers, and more than enough wineglasses to supply
the guests.[43] Ninety feet from the dining room was the separate
kitchen, a commodious one measuring thirty-two by sixteen feet
and furnished with all the pots, pans, Dutch ovens, gridirons,
frying pans, spits, griddles, and kettles necessary in a plantation
kitchen and housing also a thirty gallon and an eighty gallon
still and also two cotton wheels, a flax wheel, two looms, and
two reels. Here also were the blacksmith tools of Wheelwright
Billy.[44]

Munford's favorite room was doubtless the library. Here he
kept his collection of law books. He gave up his legal practice in
1774; nevertheless, as Justice of the Peace, Senior Magistrate, and
County Lieutenant, he still had need to refer to them. However
the section of his library which he preferred was his small but
choice library of history, poetry, fiction, and drama. Some of
the volumes he had brought from England, and here at odd
intervals he worked on his translation of Ovid's *Metamorphoses*,
begun perhaps at Wakefield, never completed, and published
with his dramas in 1798. Here also, in the 1770's, he wrote his
Candidates and his *Patriots*.

Upstairs in the hallway and the bedrooms were books for
light reading—perhaps the fiction which his daughter Elizabeth
was to know so well and quote so readily: *Gulliver's Travels*,
Candide, *Gil Blas*, *Tom Jones*, *Peregrine Pickle*, *Tristram Shandy*,
The Vicar of Wakefield. But Elizabeth quoted with equal facility
poets like Dryden, Pope, Gay, Goldsmith, and Ossian, and play-
wrights like Shakespeare and Vanbrugh.[45] Munford must have early
established the practice of family readings which William was
to find popular with his sisters: "We read a good deal to each
other, for reading is an amusement for which both my sisters
have a great taste."[46] Sleeping accommodations in the upstairs
bedrooms were usually adequate, though strained at times when

many were being entertained, as for example in 1781 when Elizabeth married and pallets were fixed on the floor.[47]

At first life together for Robert and Anna Beverley Munford
was doubtless novel and exciting, even though they had known
each other ever since Anna's babyhood; and their two daughters
must have drawn them even closer together. During these early
marital years, in order to please his young wife and place her
accouchements and convalescences among loved friends and relatives, the young couple were often at Blandfield. Munford even
shipped to the Rappahannock tobacco which he had grown 200
miles away; and for several years he seems to have continued a sort
of partnership with his brother-in-law, who thought it strange
that Munford should even after 1763 continue such a sentimental
and expensive practice.[48]

Visits to Blandfield were a delight and a joy to Anna and
the children. Years later Elizabeth remembered Blandfield, "the
haunts of my childhood and youth, with real delight; for all
about the old Manor house appears as fresh in my memory as if
I had just left it; tho' I have never seen it since the year before
Erasmus's birth. . . ."[49] Probably Richland, at least to Anna, seemed
comparatively drab. Years later, on 10 May 1808 the elder daughter
wrote Rachel Mordecai, "Oh, my dear girl, how shall I be able
to exist, in the woods and wilds of Mecklenburg . . . after being
so long in the Metropolis of the Old Dominion? heigh ho, I
suppose I shall barely breathe; for I imagine I shall be in such
a torpid state, that I shall not call it life."[50] Stoical by that time
to any retirement, Elizabeth was jesting, but her comment may
have echoed to some extent her Mother's attitude toward her
forced retirement. For Anna, Richland must have seemed drearier
as the years went by. In a review of her son's translation of the *Iliad*,
Cornelius Conway Felton characterized her as "an amiable and
accomplished lady, who added to strong natural powers the best
culture of the times, and a familiarity with the most polished
society."[51] In Southside Virginia, she must have felt even more
acutely than did her niece on the Northern Neck "that elegancies
of any sort badly become planters daughters in a republic—If
she can spin, knit or darn, she soars no higher—The Graces &
belles lettres she leaves to your monarchical ladies."[52]

Though the evidences for the impression that Robert and
Anna Munford were not completely happy together are largely
intangible ones, the plays seem to reinforce the suspicion. In
reading them one comes to feel that Munford identified himself
in *The Patriots* with Meanwell, presumably a bachelor, and in

The Candidates with Wou'dbe, whose condition may well have mirrored Munford's in family affairs as well as in political ones. In the opening scene his neighbor inquires after his "lady and family"; in Act III, scene iii, he welcomes his breakfast guests to "bachelors quarters."

In May of 1774 some local gossip seems to have been directed at Mrs. Munford. This slander need not have touched her character. Since her brother and brothers-in-law were all moderates or even tories in their sympathies, perhaps her loyalty to the American cause was suspected. At any rate, Munford acted quickly and firmly to stop loose talk, even though the principal talker was a wealthy planter with half a hundred slaves. On 14 March 1774 the slanderer, Thomas Field, publicly apologized in court: ". . . what ever he may have said derogatory to the Character of Mrs. Munfurd, was what he never intended shou'd operate to her Prejudice, and is entirely false, spoken inadvertantly, And of the greatest Contrition, for the offense that he has Committed, will obtain her Pardon he asks it in the most Submissive Terms. With which the Plaintiffs are satisfy'd and the suit is Dismissed. . . ."[53]

Perhaps this quick and determined desense of his wife led to a rapproachment. The next year their son, William, was born. But if their married life was not idyllic, they would not permit their conduct before their children to reveal any resentment. The letters of Elizabeth show clearly her veneration for the memory of both her parents and her love of her childhood memories at Richland. Writing to her friend Rachel Mordecai on 8 January 1809, she recalled:

. . . we arrived the fourth day after we began our journey at Richland and when we once more entered that Mansion, where I have passed so many halcyon days; how forcibly did every place remind me of "departed joys, departed never to return" melancholy ideas occupied my mind, for each room recalled
    'My much loved Mothers look serene,
    And all the dear enchanting scene'
when no cares perplexed me, and each day produced new pleasures; if I left the house and walked in the garden; there every thing brought my Fathers benevolent aspect before me; for that was his handy work. . . .[54]

Perhaps Anna felt neglected because her husband's multifarious activities left him little time for her and frequently took him from home. In order to set up for farming on a large scale, Munford needed some position which would furnish him with a supply of

ready money. For this reason, evidently, George Currie, as clerk
of Halifax County, deferred to his stepson and on 17 April 1760,
arranged to have Munford sworn clerk there in his stead.[55] There
was no difficulty in making the arrangement. Clerkships were practically hereditary, and Munford's friends and relatives held positions
of leadership in the county: his Uncle Richard Bland, for example,
was County Lieutenant.[56] Moreover his legal studies with Peyton
Randolph qualified him for the post. But the position was for
Munford, as it had been for Currie, a sinecure: on the third
Thursday of the month Munford theoretically attended court, but
the duties actually devolved upon William Wright, Currie's deputy
and Munford's until 19 May 1763, when Wright was replaced
by Thomas Tunstall.[57] Not only could duties be discharged by
deputy; fees were lucrative. In 1763, for example, they were
considerably in excess of £335.[58]

   Well qualified for the practice of law by his studies with the
King's Attorney and perhaps by occasional practice as Currie's
substitute, Munford, upon making his home in Lunenburg County,
recorded a license to practice as an attorney, and during the following year he seems to have qualified in Amelia County as well.[59]
His legal practice was evidently never very extensive; and it
was concerned almost exclusively with civil cases. He also frequently acted as surety or assignee; and on 27 October 1764
he was given power of attorney by William Byrd III to take
charge of all his property and financial interests in Halifax and
Lunenburg Counties.[60] Byrd's holdings in Southside Virginia were
at that time still extensive, but revenue from the position must have
been negligible: Byrd was already insolvent. But because fees were
established by law, in order to support himself by legal practice,
Munford would have been forced to exhibit a tireless energy in
several counties. He evidently felt that the return was inadequate;
and as his financial position was gradually stabilized, he began to
restrict his private practice and to devote his legal talents entirely
to the service of his country.

   As a gentleman planter, Munford was expected to take an
active part in community leadership. One of his first civic responsibilities was that of vestryman in the newly organized parish
of St. James. On 7 July 1761 he took and subscribed the oath as
vestryman. Since by 9 February 1778 he headed the list of vestrymen, he evidently performed his duties faithfully.[61]

   Munford also served as field officer in the militia. Producing
a commission from Lieutenant Governor Francis Fauquier, who
three years earlier had authorized his commission as a young

lieutenant, on 7 July 1761 Munford took the oath as Lieutenant Colonel of Lunenburg County.[62] As general musters were held only once a year, the duties of militia officers were not arduous or onerous. Since Lunenburg was no longer a frontier county, the only danger it felt lay not in the distant Indians, but in the increasing throngs of Negroes; and the only active duty for which the militia were called upon was the patrolling of the roads and countryside during periods when Negro uprisings were feared, as when Munford's Jack created "the late disturbances among the negroes."[63]

Because of his financial and social position as a large landowner and his legal training and his experience as attorney and clerk of Halifax County, young Munford was soon recommended by the County Court of Lunenburg County as a fit and able gentleman to discharge another civic duty—that of Justice of the Peace and member of the county commission. On 8 December 1763 he took the oath as Justice;[64] and for practically the rest of his life he was on the commission, first, of Lunenburg, then of Mecklenburg County. His duties in this capacity, again, were not particularly demanding. Over and above his attendance at court he had to decide, as Justice of the Peace, small financial suits involving less than 7/6 and to keep the peace in his district. Court met only once a month, though sometimes the docket required two or even three days' attendance. Moreover it was evidently a gentleman's agreement that attendance was to be so spaced that no member of the commission, whether he was of the quorum or not, would find his time unduly taxed. Munford was present approximately half the time; frequently he arrived late, and sometimes he left early. But if duties were not onerous, his position threw him into a position of local prominence, for court days were festive occasions in Colonial Virginia, and those seated on the bench in the wainscotted court room received attention and respect from the holiday audiences.

Munford's rise into local notice had indeed been rapid, but in 1765 he came into more general prominence. By an act of the General Assembly of October, 1764, a new county, Mecklenburg, was created from the southern half of Lunenburg County; and from the very first Munford was one of the prime movers in setting up the apparatus of county government. On 21 December 1764 he was appointed Senior Magistrate, heading the list of justices slated for the county commission; and at the very first meeting of that body, on 11 March 1765, he produced Fauquier's commission appointing him County Lieutenant.[65]

As County Lieutenant of Mecklenburg County Munford was responsible for training and equipping an effective militia. He had seen enough of military life in his capacity as Byrd's captain-lieutenant to enable him capably to discharge his new duties; and his late experience as Lieutenant Colonel of the Lunenburg militia was helpful.

Just as demanding as his military duties were his civil responsibilities. Members of the commission of the newly created county were faced with many tasks demanding time, intelligence, and energy. As a leading citizen, county lieutenant, and a gentleman learned in law he was called upon frequently. He was for example one of the four commissioners, along with Paul Carrington, William Taylor, and Clement Read, appointed to settle among Mecklenburg, Charlotte, and Lunenburg counties the claims due the county of Lunenburg before the separation of Mecklenburg from the parent county.[66] Less than a year later, on 14 July 1766 he was appointed Agent, or Treasurer for Mecklenburg County, to "Settle with the Collector and render an Account at the laying of the County Levy Yearly."[67]

Upon the formation of Mecklenburg County, Munford was chosen, along with Edmund Taylor, to represent it as one of its burgesses. Thus he was sent to the House of Burgesses in Williamsburg as had been his father and his grandfather before him. In five short years he had risen to be one of the most prominent leaders of Southside Virginia.

~~~ III ~~~

Virginia Burgess

ALTHOUGH Mecklenburg County remained the scene of most of his activities, his election in 1765 to the House of Burgesses meant that until the Revolution, unless political affairs were merely routine or unless business at home were so pressing that it demanded his presence, Munford spent a considerable and important part of the year at Williamsburg. Here he was to play a part in the shaping of the American Revolution.

When he arrived there, at the end of May, 1765, Williamsburg looked rather different from the small provincial town where he had studied law from 1756 until 1760. The outstanding features were still the same as when they were described, a few years before, by Andrew Burnaby:

It consists of about two hundred houses, does not contain more than one thousand souls, whites and negroes. . . . It is regularly laid out in parallel streets, intersected by others at right angles; has a handsome square in the center, through which runs the principal street, one of the most spacious in North America, three quarters of a mile in length, and above a hundred feet wide. At the opposite ends of this street are two public buildings, the college and the capitol: and although the houses are of wood, covered with shingles, and but indifferently built, the whole makes a handsome appearance. . . . The governor's palace is tolerably good, one of the best upon the continent; but the church, the prison, and the other buildings, are all of them extremely indifferent. The streets are not paved, and are consequently very dusty. . . . Upon the whole, it is an agreeable residence; there are ten or twelve gentlemen's families constantly residing in it, besides merchants and tradesmen: and at the times of the assemblies, and general courts, it is crowded with the gentry of the country: on those occasions there are balls and other amusements; but as soon as the business is finished, they return to their plantations; and the town is in a manner deserted.[1]

Within these few years since Munford's student days some changes had taken place: the city limits had been twice extended, and the resident population now stood at perhaps two thousand.

25

From the Bruton Parish Church there now pealed occasionally a
bell, acquired in 1761.[2] But the main difference was that the
town was now far from deserted. A French visitor who preceded
Munford by a few days complained of a throng of five or six
thousand: "on our arival we had great Difficulty to get lodgings
but thanks to mr sprowl I got a room at mrs. vaubes's tavern,
where all the best people resorted. I soon got acquainted with
severals of them, but particularly with Colonel Burd, sir peton
skiper . . . which I soon was like to have had reason to repent, for
they are all professed gamesters, Especially Colonel Burd, who is
never happy but when he has the box and Dices in hand. this
Gentleman from a man of the greatest property of any in america
has reduced himself to that Degree by gameing, that few or nobody
will Credit him for Ever so small a sum of money."[3] It was
doubtless to this tavern kept by Mrs. Jane Vaube that Munford
came when he arrived in Williamsburg. There, at any rate, he
would have found congenial company in his old friend William
Byrd III and in Sir Peyton Skipwith.

On his very first recorded appearance in the House of Burgesses, young Munford took his stand as a defender of Colonial
liberties. Immediately he aligned himself with the young and
liberal group to support Patrick Henry, a young burgess from
Louisa County who was, like himself, serving his first term as a
burgess. Munford was among a slim group of thirty-nine when on
the fateful day 29 May 1765 Henry rose and presented to the
Committee of the Whole House his resolutions protesting against
the Stamp Act. The following day he was more than a thrilled
supporter when Henry spoke for his resolutions and maintained that
the colonists possessed all the rights and privileges of English
citizens, demanded for Virginia its birthright of self-taxation, and
asserted that any attempt to vest this power elsewhere tended to
destroy British as well as American freedom. For Munford was
one of the three colleagues who had been with Henry "in Con-
clave, at Lewis, Consulting & preparing resolutions upon that
Subject"; and the resolutions may indeed owe as much to Munford
as to Henry himself.[4] Young Munford must have been disappointed
when his uncle Richard Bland spoke against the resolutions, as
did his mentor Peyton Randolph, who was reported willing to
give as much as £100 for a single opposing vote.[5] But as soon
as Munford was able to collect himself, he rose to support Henry.[6]
Thereby he numbered himself among "the Young, hot and Giddy
Members," as Fauquier termed them.[7] Henry left the next day,
presuming that since his resolutions had been adopted by the

House, his work was for the time accomplished. But the conservatives attempted to expunge them from the record. Munford must have helped to defend the resolutions; and it is to the credit of Henry's outspoken young adherents that they successfully defended four.

Not only did Munford play a prominent part in the passage of the resolutions. When a day or so later the House adjourned and he returned home, he helped to implement Henry's resolutions by keeping the courts of Mecklenburg County closed not only during the customary month of January, but through December, February, and March as well, and keeping the Halifax courts closed even longer, bringing legal transactions in these counties to a halt in protest against the Stamp Act and thus delaying all suits for debt by British merchants against the colonists.

Repeal of the Stamp Act, however, not only dampened the spirit of protest in the Virginians, but it even brought about a reaction in favor of loyalism. Such opposition as developed during the year 1766 came outside the House of Burgesses. A few days before news of the repeal reached Williamsburg, Munford's uncle Richard Bland published there perhaps the most important pamphlet of the Revolution—*An Inquiry into the Rights of the British Colonies*. Herein Bland defended the principles violated by the Stamp Act and affirmed the independence of Virginia from the British Parliament: only to the King himself, Bland asserted, did Virginia owe obedience.

The 1766 session was indeed calm, or routine in comparison with the brief session in which Munford had just served his noviciate. When he arrived at Williamsburg he found that a major concern was the form which Colonial gratitude should assume. He was named on a committee instructed to prepare "Inscriptions for the Obelisk" to commemorate the patriots in Parliament who had been instrumental in the repeal of the Stamp Act.[8] He was witness at the outset to a contest for the speakership, vacated by the death of Speaker Robinson, when his uncle Richard Bland was nominated by Richard Henry Lee to oppose cousin Peyton Randolph. The successful Randolph appointed Munford to two important committees: on 7 November 1766 Munford was named on the Committee of Propositions and Grievances, a standing committee of considerable power; and on 28 November, on the committee of fifteen to remove the seat of government to some more convenient place.[9] He also served on or headed some of the numerous small committees which docked the entail on landed estates. These duties were perhaps designed to make use of the legal training and abilities of a young and willing member, to bring him forward into the notice of the other burgesses, and to give him training and experience under the supervision of the older members. Interest of the 1766 session was again heightened by the presence of old friends like John Banister, Robert Bolling, and William Byrd, who was a member of the Governor's Council, and numerous relatives: uncles Richard Bland and Henry Lee, cousins Peyton Randolph and Robert Munford of Amelia.

During the session of 1767, which lasted from 12 March until 11 April, relationships with the Mother Country continued calm. In domestic affairs, however, the Robinson scandal, revealed during the previous session, was causing considerable embarrassment and indignation. Treasurer as well as Speaker, Robinson had misappropriated public funds by secretly lending them to private individuals. Munford was certainly concerned about the affair, for Byrd was by far the largest debtor to the Robinson estate, and Munford was not only Byrd's friend but his legal and financial representative for a large part of Southside Virginia.[10]

The year 1768 was financially quite difficult for Munford. He was sued for a debt of £600 by Peter Jones, Jr., and judgment went against him.[11] During the same year he was sued by Thomas Starke for debt; and even though the amount was the comparatively small one of £10/3/11, Munford was driven to the embarrassing expedient of pleading prior payment. Later he gave up this plea and admitted liability.[12] His need for cash may have prompted him to give up property in Mecklenburg County in a lottery scheme with several other prominent planters of Southside Virginia, like Clement and Isaac Read, Paul Carrington, Matthew Marrable, Henry Deloney, William Taylor, and cousin Thomas Jefferson, of Albemarle.[13]

Despite these financial reverses, however, and the absence again of his name from the scanty journals recording the brief session, he probably attended the session, arriving late and departing early.[14] He would have felt it his duty to oppose the Revenue Act of 1767, which replaced the Stamp Act. He probably shared the concern of the other burgesses over the treatment of Massachusetts and New York and voted with the rest to assert Virginia's right to self-taxation. Moreover pleasure beckoned to Williamsburg as well as duty, for during the months of February through April the Virginia Company of Players was acting there.

The years 1769 and 1770, which saw a resurgence of resistance to England, certainly saw Munford on the floor of the House. During the short, May session of 1769 he was especially busy.

He was present on the opening day of 8 May 1769 and doubtless helped to welcome, with traditional pomp and ceremony, the new Governor, the Right Honorable Norbone Berkeley, Baron de Botetourt. On the same day he was appointed, along with Thomas Jefferson, the new burgess from Albemarle, and others, to the important standing committees of Propositions and Grievances and Privileges and Elections, where he was kept busy by an unusual amount of work.[15] But the House had to consider matters far more important than even the most importune domestic issues. On 16 May, Munford was present when the Committee of the Whole House reaffirmed *nemine contradicente* the right of the American colonists to levy their own taxes, affirmed the right of the colonists to trial in Virginia rather than overseas, no matter what the charge might be, and asserted the right of Virginians to petition the Throne directly.[16] After these resolutions were passed unanimously by the House, Botetourt dissolved it. Munford was among those who assembled on 18 May at the Raleigh Tavern and signed the Articles of the Williamsburg Association, pledging the signers not to import or purchase merchandise from England until the hated duties on tea and paper were repealed.[17]

A few days later, on 22 May 1769, his brother, Theoderick, signed a marriage bond to enable him to marry Frances Moseley, of Princess Anne County, perhaps the same Frances Moseley for whom on 11 November 1763 James Hunter, Jr. had signed a similar bond.[18] Evidently this preliminary also failed to be consummated in marriage.

When the House of Burgesses met in November, 1769, Munford again attended, arriving late, on 11 November, with his colleague Matthew Marrable. The Virginians expected a determined struggle with his Majesty's Governor. No such struggle developed; Botetourt was able, on the authority of the Earl of Hillsborough, then Secretary of State, to reassure the colonists that the duties of which they complained so bitterly would soon be repealed. Interest in this session subsequently centered upon the western extension of Virginia's border. Munford himself was busy on the standing committees to which he had already been appointed in the previous session. On 25 November he requested and secured permission to absent himself from the House until 15 December.[19] Why he left is not clear. Perhaps he was canvassing his constituents in Mecklenburg County to ascertain exactly their attitude towards the ferriage bill which he had seen through a previous session and which was, as a result of a Mecklenburg petition, the target of a move to rescind. At any rate, he was back at his committee duties by 21 December, when he was appointed chairman of a sub-committee or commission to inquire into the conduct of Nathaniel Terry, burgess from Halifax.[20]

When the adjourned session met 21 May 1770, Munford was present. There was little important business transacted; but as chairman of the commission to examine the conduct of Terry, Munford had the uncomfortable duty of making public a detailed censure. The most important revolutionary action was again taken outside the House of Burgesses, with the formation of a new Association. Directed at the failure of the British Parliament to lift the hated duties on tea, it was designed not only to bind its signers but to affect all Virginians by the machinery of committees of five set up in each county to publish the names of offenders and to recommend merchants who cooperated with the program of boycott. This organization, sponsored by the Cape Company of Merchants, including merchant captain Theoderick Munford, numbered many prominent burgesses among its leaders. Munford, like George Washington, remained over until 22 June to sign. The next day he received permission to absent himself for the remainder of the session. Two days later he was probably present when Theoderick purchased the ancestral Whitehall, now reduced to 711 acres, from their mother and their sister, Elizabeth McRobert.

Their mother died early in February, 1771. Step-father George Currie had probably made all the funeral arrangements before Munford arrived from Richland. Theoderick, who had remained closest to her, may have been at that time on one of his regular voyages to Bristol. But Elizabeth was probably present; and certainly at the funeral were the half-sisters Anna Currie, later a correspondent of her cousin Frances Randolph, and Margaret. Perhaps Margaret had already married her first husband, John Fawn, captain of the *Prince George*, and had with her her son John, later himself a captain and an acquaintance of Munford's daughter Elizabeth.[21]

Whether Munford attended the sessions of 1771, 1772, and 1773 the scanty journals of the House of Burgesses do not reveal; it seems unlikely that he attended regularly. During this period the spirit of rebellion was not fervent in Virginia. The brief, special session of 1771, called by President Nelson, was devoted largely to the relief of those who were suffering as a result of the spring floods; and the similarly brief session of 1773 was concerned mainly with measures designed to stop counterfeiting. Other colonies were experiencing their difficulties with the Mother Country, and Virginia occasionally voiced its sympathies with their sufferings. But after the death of Governor Botetourt in October, 1770, and the arrival in the fall of 1771 of the new governor, John Murray, Earl of Dunmore, Virginia was for a while placated by a diplomat who centered attention upon domestic improvements, which the colony badly needed.

During these years Munford was perhaps diverted from his duties at Williamsburg by a series of financial and personal misfortunes. On 26 May 1771 the Great Fresh on the Roanoke severely damaged his property and inundated a considerable part of his fields. The year 1772 was even more unfortunate. The price of tobacco was falling: it was to reach a low of 12/6 by midsummer of 1773. Then on 11 March the House of Burgesses, Munford evidently absent, on being informed that the Clerk of Halifax County had not sent in his list of tithables, ordered that a list be secured at his expense.[22] The immediate penalty to Munford was not the main cost, however, for Thomas Tunstall, Munford's deputy, was forced to underwrite this.[23] But early the following year Munford was relieved of his clerkship. The practice of absentee clerkship was not the issue; although Paul Carrington, who replaced Munford as clerk of Halifax on 21 January 1773,[24] was legally required after his appointment to resign his seat in the House, he was immediately re-elected and continued to serve as burgess for Charlotte and clerk for Halifax. Nor was the blame put upon Munford's deputy, Thomas Tunstall: he was retained at his post by Carrington. Munford's dismissal may have been intended to remedy a breakdown in communications between Halifax County and Williamsburg. Munford evidently attended neither the sessions of 1771 nor 1772; and because there was no sheriff to execute the writ, no burgesses had been returned for Halifax for the 1772 session.[25] Moreover it must have been somewhat embarrassing for Munford, after his damning report on the dishonesty of Terry, to continue to serve as clerk in a county which gave Terry a clear vote of confidence by re-electing him to the House of Burgesses. Evidently Munford became almost desperate and went to Williamsburg to try to mend financial and political fences. Writing to Theoderick Munford from Williamsburg on 16 May 1772, Matthew Phipps suggested that Robert was not averse to using Theoderick's credits to balance some of his own pressing debts.[26] So difficult, indeed, did Munford's financial position become about this time that he even resumed the practice of law, qualifying in Mecklenburg County on 14 September 1772 and in Halifax County on 18 February 1773, less than a month after he was replaced as clerk.[27]

Personal difficulties also harrassed Munford. On 10 March, the day after the House called for the Halifax list, Munford's neighbor and colleague Matthew Marrable, because of a dispute concerning their boundaries, refused to permit their lines to be processioned, in the annual walking of property lines. Perhaps it was this very dispute which led Marrable to ask leave to absent himself from the House from 4 March until 15 March.[28] Finally, on 8 October came the news that Munford's only brother, Captain Theoderick Munford, had died.[29]

This personal loss was for Munford somewhat alleviated by his receiving periodically sums which permitted him ultimately to resign his legal practice. Since the estate was not finally settled until after March, 1777, Munford continued to practice law, until 11 April 1774.[30] But some time before 13 July 1773 he ordered a post chaise from Norton in London, and in September, 1773, he was again buying land, seemingly with an expanding economy.[31]

For the brief session of May, 1774, Munford arrived late, on 16 May, the same day as Marrable and the representatives from Halifax—Coles and Terry. Perhaps there had been some reconciliation. Munford was immediately appointed to his customary assignments on the committees of Privileges and Elections and Propositions and Grievances.[32] Suddenly, on 26 May, Lord Dunmore, angered by the proclamation of a day of fasting and prayer to signalize the resolutions of sympathy with Boston, dissolved the House. Munford retired with the rest to Raleigh Tavern and on 27 May signed the Association, which adopted a boycott on tea, deplored the British attack upon their brothers in Boston, and suggested a General Continental Congress.[33]

Two months later, on 29 July, Munford presided over a meeting of the freeholders of Mecklenburg as they approved the resolutions of the Association. They rejected taxation except that passed by the colony itself and expressed sympathy with Boston. The freeholders asserted their personal allegiance to the King but insisted that as British subjects all were entitled to his protection of their unabridged civil rights. In protesting taxation without representation, they insisted that they would "contend for this inestimable privilege, at the Hazard" of their "Lives and Fortunes."[34]

When the First Virginia Convention met at Williamsburg on 1 August 1774, Munford was evidently present. It was an occasion of such importance that few of the delegates, most of them regularly elected members of the House of Burgesses, chose to be absent.[35] He must have readily voted for the resolve to send delegates to the General Congress to be held soon in Philadelphia; and he must have had no radical objection to the decision to cease all English imports on 1 November; but when debate opened on the resolution to stop all exports to England, even tobacco, he doubtless aligned himself with the conservative group headed by Paul Carrington in opposition to this measure.[36] The already half-grown tobacco, he realized, must be shipped so that debts could be paid. Both as lawyer and planter, Munford must have supported the conservatives who successfully delayed the export provision for a year, to take effect if by that time England had not redressed all American grievances.

Munford's reluctance, for financial, legal, and probably sentimental reasons, for a final, definite break with the Mother Country can be seen in a letter which he wrote, on 20 April 1775, to his loyalist friend William Byrd III:

Your Account of public Matters is little more than the Effects of those unwarrantable Measures that have been adopted with too much Precipitation by our unwary Countrymen. Our present Difficulties only presage Calamaties more poynant hereafter. The Train of Miseries consequential of the intemperate Warmth displayed by the people here, are too apparent. Nothing I am fearful can now avert the Evils of a civil War. However I am determined to make one Effort more to bring those immediately under my Observation, to a due Sense of the Obligations both of Duty and Allegiance that bind them to their Soverign, and to the Preservation of civil Order. I have drawn up an Address to the Governor, which I am in Hopes the moderate and prudent will agree to, solely to declare to his Excellency that their Intentions are peaceable and upright and that it is and shall be their Aim carefully to avoid all such Conduct as may tend to throw the State into civil Commotion. Denying that they approve the Spirit for Warfare displayed by the last Convention, that they will not embody or arm untill required by the constituent Powers of the Legislature or the Comander in Chief, and promising by no Overt Act to contravene that Regularity of Duty which their Faith to the King and a due Submission to the Laws of their Country may exact from them. If I can carry the Point for such an Address, it will be no bad Proof of the good Disposition of the people in Mecklenburg. As our Loyalty begins to be suspected, it is high Time to speak out. . . .[37]

Before this time, as can be inferred from this letter, local political leadership had passed from Munford to the county committee for the enforcement of the Association, a committee chaired by John Speed.[38] Except for criminal cases, county courts had been practically closed since May, 1774, when Dunmore, by dissolving the assembly, prevented that body from providing for the proper legal functioning of these courts. Accordingly, on 13 June 1774 in the Mecklenburg Court it was "Ordered that the Court be adjourned untill Court in fouse [force]." The Mecklenburg Court continued to meet, and it continued to concern itself with roads and financial matters as well as with criminal cases; but from 13 February 1775 this body evidently became dominated by John Speed and other members of the Committee of Safety. The break between Colonial Virginia and Revolutionary Virginia became steadily more pronounced. On 13 February 1775 Robert Williams was authorized to purchase land for a new county seat; and on the same day, with Speed presiding, the court began to reverse some of its earlier decisions concerning debts to the British and Scottish factors.[39] When the delegates were elected to the Second Virginia Convention, which met 20 March 1775, Mecklenburg County was represented by Robert Burton and Bennett Goode, men who had never even been recommended for the county commission. In May they were given a vote of thanks for their services by the committee of freeholders formed "to secure a due observation of the association," and at the Third Virginia Convention, which met in July, they again represented Mecklenburg.

Meanwhile, at Williamsburg Munford was inevitably driven from his position of compromise to one of resistance as he played a prominent part in the struggle between Governor Dunmore and the burgesses. When Dunmore convoked the House of Burgesses on 1 June 1775, he wished to pacify the Virginians by presenting the conciliatory proposals of Lord North. But earlier, on the night of 20-21 April, he had made the mistake of removing powder belonging to the Colony from the public magazine at Williamsburg. The Virginians were at once alarmed and aroused. Patrick Henry led a company of volunteers toward Williamsburg, and another company started. Alarmed in return, Dunmore declared Henry an outlaw, fortified the Palace, and put his wife and children aboard the *Fowey*.[41] Thus the session opened under feelings of mutual suspicion and distrust. Recognizing the gravity of the situation, Thomas Jefferson and Peyton Randolph, although they were delegates to the Continental Congress and indeed Randolph was chairman, went not to Philadelphia, but to Williamsburg. As burgesses they felt their presence demanded at this crucial time, and Randolph was still Speaker of the House.

From the outset of the session a series of controversies divided the Governor and the burgesses. Was the public magazine actually unsafe and the removal of powder thus justified? What really caused the popular uprisings that followed this removal? In view of these disturbances, was the person of the Governor really safe in Williamsburg? At times these issues obscured or at least obfuscated the central issue: were North's proposals adequate to satisfy Virginia?

Among the fifteen committees named to represent the House in these disputes, Munford was pressed into service on nine. Various committees, always with a central core of constituents— the Treasurer, Mercer, Cary, Jones, and Munford—were kept busy drafting resolutions, addresses, and replies, conferring with the Council representatives, and attending Dunmore at the Palace and subsequently on board the *Fowey*. When Dunmore opened the session and presented North's proposals, Munford was appointed to the committee to consider them. Here he worked with Thomas Jefferson as Jefferson drafted a firm address which defended the colonists for their closing the courts and protested against the action of Parliament in cutting off all foreign trade.[42] On 5 June Munford was named to the Committee "to inspect the public Magazine" and "inquire into the Stores thereof." This group waited on Dunmore for his report, but was finally forced to strong language to secure the key to the magazine. Dunmore refused to restore the powder. The committee discovered other depredations, and on 17 June Munford became a member of a Joint Committee of the House and Council to address Dunmore concerning the locks removed from the guns in the magazine.[43] Meanwhile Munford was appointed to the committee instructed to entreat Dunmore to reconsider his threat to withdraw from the city.[44] This plea and later ones had no effect; Dunmore answered that the spirit of lawlessness exhibited by the colonists threatened his very life. Thus charges and countercharges flew between the Governor and the House, and though at times each tried to be conciliatory, the disputes developed rapidly until the House and the Governor reached an impasse. Dunmore demanded to no avail that the burgesses attend him on board the *Fowey* to secure his assent to the enrolled bills. After that, neither side could compromise. The Revolution in Virginia had begun.

~~IV~~

Delegate and Soldier

THUS as a Virginia burgess, Munford played his part in the Colonial protest against British autocracy. During the Revolution he was to play an even more important role in the Virginia legislature and in the militia.

After the final adjournment of the House of Burgesses, the Revolutionary Convention at Richmond began, in July, 1775, preparing to resist the expected British challenge. It authorized the enlistment of only two regiments of regulars—a small force of 1020 privates and their officers.[1] Virginia expected to rely for its defense mainly upon a well-trained force of minutemen. The new militia laws provided that these would not receive the some-times merely nominal training given the regular militia, but would be formed into battalions and given battalion training for twenty successive days upon embodiment and twelve successive days twice each year thereafter. In addition, each company would receive unit training for four successive days each month, except during the winter. Such at least was the ambitious program.[2] Regular militia training also was intensified under the July laws. Instead of one general muster a year, there were to be two, in April and October; and musters of each company were to be held every fortnight except during the winter.[3] The regular militia and the minutemen were placed under the supervision of the Virginia Committee of Public Safety; and the officers, including even the county lieuten-ants, were to be nominated by the local committees.[4]

Although many of the local freeholders distrusted Munford's conservatism in politics and had not even named him among the twenty-one members of the Mecklenburg Committee, that body respected his experience in military matters and his performance as county lieutenant; he was, therefore, retained at that responsible post. As county lieutenant in charge of all military affairs, Munford began to enlist men for the regular army and to train and equip minutemen and regular militia for active duty whenever they might be ordered out. Under his direction recruitment went forward rapidly. Captain Robert Ballard's company, raised in the Mecklenburg area, was in Williamsburg by 21 October 1775;[5] and another company of regulars to include a strong contingent from Mecklenburg, James Johnston's, was embodied and in service before 1 November 1775.[6] Recruitment ceased to be entirely Munford's responsibility when the December Convention ordered that recruitment of six additional regular regiments would be handled in the counties by a captain and other officers appointed by the county committee.[7] But in raising Samuel Hopkins' company, assigned to the Sixth Regiment, Munford was given ultimate authority.[8]

The minutemen of Mecklenburg County were especially active. When on 18 February 1776 North Carolina was threatened with an invasion, Edmund Pendleton wrote reassuringly for the Virginia Committee of Public Safety to Colonel Long, in North Carolina: ". . . we can only assist you in men from Militia or Volunteers from the counties bordering on you, all of whom we are persuaded, you will find ready to afford you any assistance in their powers from Pitsylvania and Mecklenburg, we had rec'd intimations of their expecting such a call and inclination to go to your assistance, and had our orders to be ready for a march, when you called for them."[9] Before 13 June Captain John Ballard's minutemen were ordered to North Carolina; but since the danger there proved only temporary, the company was dispatched to Williamsburg at the request of Governor Patrick Henry for troops to defend that city. Stationed at Hampton and later at Portsmouth during this same summer were companies of Mecklenburg minutemen under the command of Captains Henry Deloney, Jr. and James Anderson.[10]

Major changes in the military and legal systems were made by the Convention of May, 1776. Recommendations for the appointment of militia officers were now taken out of the hands of the county committees and restored to the county courts.[11] Still excluding lawsuits concerning debts, these were now reopened throughout the state; they had remained open in Mecklenburg.

Aside from his duties as County Lieutenant and Senior Magistrate officiating at the county court, Munford for several years, until May of 1779, led a comparatively ordered life, and it was during this period that he had the leisure to write *The Patriots*. Invasion threatened occasionally; and in 1777 companies of minutemen were twice summoned to active duty, on 16 August when Williamsburg was threatened and again in November and December when North Carolina requested help.[12] Otherwise life subsided into a regular round of planting, hoeing, and harvesting, with rumors of distant wars and occasional threats of invasion. Virginians began to feel secure. As early as May, 1776, the Virginia Convention had listened sympathetically to protests of the minutemen that the rigorous schedule of training was inconvenient and protests of the militia that fortnightly company meetings were too taxing. These were now reduced to a meeting no more frequent than once every four weeks.[13]

Munford's thorough and conscientious service in preparing Mecklenburg for warfare gradually rehabilitated him with the freeholders as a loyal and patriotic Virginian. Increased trust in his reliability appeared in 1777 when, on 14 July and 11 August, he was designated one of the justices directed to make the tour of the county and administer the oath of loyalty.[14] To the Virginia Conventions, Mecklenburg freeholders had sent Bennett Goode, Robert Burton, and Joseph Speed. In the House of Delegates they had been represented by Joseph Speed, Bennett and Samuel Goode, and Henry Deloney. In the election of early 1779, however, the freeholders again gave Munford a vote of confidence; they elected him to represent them in the House of Delegates as he had for years represented them in the House of Burgesses.

When Munford took his seat in the House of Delegates, in May, 1779, he enjoyed a position of confidence and even eminence. During the term he was named to numerous committees, some of them routine, but others quite important. These committee responsibilities necessitated a familiarity with and entailed a responsibility for far-reaching civilian and military problems.

On 11 May 1779, presumably the day of his arrival, he was named, with Jefferson and George Mason, to serve on the committee to establish a Land Office for granting "waste and unappropriated lands," particularly for the benefit of veterans.[15] Familiar by this time with the situation in the Western Lands, he was subsequently named, on 31 May, to the committee charged to consider a letter from the Virginia delegates in Congress concerning "certain proceedings of the General Assembly of Maryland, respecting the confederation," i.e., advocating the grant to large landholding companies of areas which subsequently became entire states.[16] Virginia had already, in 1776 and in the fall of 1778, made quite clear that it would not recognize any private, unrecorded purchase of Indian lands. But there was continual pressure to do so not only from outside forces like the Indiana and Vandalia companies, but from within by interested delegates like George

Mason, who wanted the privilege for his own Ohio Company. On 9 June 1779 the House reiterated its stand, but on 29 October Congress asked Virginia to reconsider and to open a Land Office.[17] For his committee, headed originally by Jefferson, Munford presented on 13 November 1779 the resolution: "That a remonstrance be drawn up to the Hon. the American Congress, firmly asserting the rights of this Commonwealth to its own territory, complaining of their having received petitions from certain persons, styling themselves the Indiana and Vandalia companies, upon claims which not only interfere with their laws and internal policy, but tend to subvert the government of this Commonwealth, and introduce general confusion; and expressly excepting and protesting against the jurisdiction of Congress therein, as unwarranted by the fundamental principles of the confederation."[18] This strong report led to Munford's nomination as chairman of a committee with Mason and Henry to prepare and bring in a remonstrance to this effect, and on 10 December this committee reasserted Virginia's sole right to dispose of its western lands.[19]

Munford was also named, apparently on the day of his arrival, to the Committee for Establishing a Board of Trade, along with Jefferson and Tyler.[20] This board was designed to act as a supply board, to procure, largely by importation, military and essential civilian supplies, and possessed wide powers, subject only to executive control.

A few weeks later, on 2 June 1779, when Virginia began to attempt to provide its own munitions, he was named, along with Jefferson, Henry, Tyler, and Mason, to the important committee to consider the petition of Penet, Wendell, and Co., regarding the founding of an army manufactory at Westham.[21] Unfortunately progress was slow, as Mason complained in a letter of 19 June to R. H. Lee: "We have had Mr. Pinet and Co.'s memorial several days before a select committee, the members of which seem well inclined to encourage so important an undertaking; if this can properly be said of men who are too indolent to attend to anything. The committee have met, or rather failed to meet, at my lodgings every morning and evening for this fortnight. Ballendine has got possession of the key to the navigation of James River, and is acting exactly the part of the dog in the manger. I am very uneasy about it, and fearful nothing decisive will be done. . . ."[22] Quite naturally Bellendine countered Penet by presenting a petition protesting against taking away his privileges. On 14 June Munford was appointed to serve on the committee to consider this petition also, since the two com-

mittees were considering different aspects of one important problem—a problem extremely vexatious to Jefferson and important
to the Commonwealth and the Confederation.[23]

Earlier, on 13 May, Munford was given his most important
committee assignment of the session—that as chairman of a committee, including Jefferson, to bring in a bill "for the better regula-
tion and discipline of the militia," an appointment which recognized the thoroughness with which Munford had built up the
Mecklenburg militia.[24] Still earlier, on 2 June, he had been named
to the committee to augment the military forces of the state by
raising 2500 volunteers and 1500 militia for the better defense
of the Commonwealth.[25]

Even while the Militia Bill was being considered, the prestige
of the Virginia militia in general and of Munford's Mecklenburg
militia in particular had been enhanced by the action at Stono
Ferry, South Carolina, whither a brigade of Southside militia had
marched under the command of Colonel David Mason. Mason's
brigade included Captain Reuben Vaughn's company of Mecklenburg militia, originally drafted for two months service in January
of 1779. On 10 June some of Vaughn's men took part in a scouting
party which captured two small vessels on the Stono River. The
next day the American commander, General Anthony Lincoln,
ordered an attack upon the British position.[26] Partly because of
General William Moultrie's negligence and the flight of some of
the South Carolina militia, however, the attack failed, and Lincoln
ordered a general retreat, recorded by Lighthorse Harry Lee:

> This movement produced now . . . some disorder; which being
> perceived by Maitland, he advanced upon Lincoln with his whole
> force. The cavalry . . . were ordered up by the American general
> to charge the enemy, whose zeal in pursuit had thrown them into loose
> order. This was gallantly executed; but Maitland closed his ranks as
> the horse bore upon him, and giving them a full fire from his rear
> rank, the front, holding its ground with charged bayonets, brought
> this corps (brave but undisciplined) to the right about. Mason, with
> his Virginia brigade, now advanced, delivering a heavy fire. The
> enemy drew back; and our retreat was effected in tolerable order.[27]

When the House of Delegates reconvened in October of 1779,
Munford occupied a position of respect and influence. Soon after
his arrival he was placed on three important standing committees—
those of Propositions and Grievances, Privileges and Elections, and
Courts of Justice.[28] Somewhat later, on 10 November 1779, he
was elected by ballot as one of the seven members of the powerful
Ways and Means Committee.[29]

In addition to serving on these standing committees, he headed or served on committees working in quite varied fields: religion and morality, travel, finance, law, and military affairs. On 15 October, he was named on the ineffectual committee instructed to bring in a bill concerning religion. On the same day he was appointed to a more successful, small committee to prepare legislation to control ordinaries and tippling houses.[30] On 18 October he was appointed chairman of a committee to suppress gambling.[31] Viewed in Colonial Virginia as a gentleman's privilege, it was more strictly regarded by the Commonwealth. Thus on 19 October the House received from Culpeper County a petition deploring the evils of gaming and "praying that a law may pass declaring that all persons under fifty years of age who shall play or bet at any kind of game, shall be deemed soldiers for two years, and all persons above that age, who are guilty thereof, be obligated to pay double taxes."[32] The petition was referred to Munford's committee, and early in December an amended bill became law. Although it did not quite satisfy the Culpeper petition, it was drastic enough. All promises to pay on bets laid on any sort of wager were henceforth to be void, whether the game were cards, dice, backgammon, bowls, horseracing, or cockfighting. Wagering a pound or more was to disqualify the gamester from holding civil or military office for two years, and winner and loser were obligated to pay half of all bets over £5. Public gaming in tavern or racefield was to incapacitate the better from holding any public office of trust; and thenceforth lotteries were not to be permitted.[33]

One of Munford's committee appointments, of 18 October, to prepare legislation to provide for the erection of cross posts, or road signs, might seem to have been a trivial duty; but it was important enough for Jefferson to propose and to deserve the services of Randolph, Henry, and Mason, as well as Munford.[34] From his work on the Mecklenburg Court, his experience as a circuit lawyer, and his trips to Williamsburg and Essex County, Munford realized how important clear directions were for the network of roads which had become increasingly important to supplement the natural waterways of Virginia. A few days later, on 21 October, he was appointed, with Pendleton and R. H. Lee, on the inefficacious committee concerning roads, mill dams, and bridges.[35]

Far more varied was Munford's work on committees which dealt with financial and legal problems. To prepare a bill "for discouraging extensive credits, and prescribing the method of proving book debts," Mason only was designated; but he obviously asked for Munford, and when on 23 October the House resolved itself into a Committee of the Whole to consider the bill, it was Munford who read the amendments and secured its passage.[36] He was also busy on committees concerned with taxation. On 26 October he was named, along with Mason and Henry, on a committee instructed to bring in a bill "for appointing commissioners to ascertain the value of lands throughout this state."[37] On the day following he was appointed to the committee directed to prepare a circular letter to the counties concerning taxation.[38]

Bills concerning fees and salaries also occupied his time. On 9 November he was named on a committee to bring in a bill, subsequently rejected, "for regulating and collecting certain officers fees," and he was appointed to a committee to bring in a bill concerning tobacco fees.[39] Earlier, on 26 October, Patrick Henry was directed to prepare a bill "to explain and emend two several acts of the last session of General Assembly, for fixing the allowance of the members thereof." Only Henry was named, but he must have requested Munford's assistance, for on the following day Munford presented the bill, and two days later he carried it to the Senate, where it cleared without difficulty.[40] Evidently Munford had remained on good terms with Henry ever since the day Munford, in his maiden speech, supported Henry's resolves. Moreover, Henry's respect for Munford must have been generally known, for in the session of spring, 1779, Munford was appointed chairman of the committee to present resolutions of gratitude to Governor Henry.[41]

For committee assignments Munford's legal training also was called into play. On 1 November he was appointed on General Nelson's committee to bring in a bill to prevent illegal possession of lands.[42] On 19 October he had been appointed to a committee, headed by Mason and including Henry and Nelson, to examine the report that some of the Virginia sheriffs had lent public funds to individuals for speculation in the purchase of Western lands—a report found to apply only to one or two.[43] On the same day Munford was named to another committee including the same group, instructed to emend the "act, concerning escheats and forfeitures from British subjects." Before this committee was discharged, Munford presented a subcommittee report on the petition of John Baylor, and this report made more lenient the final version of the emended law.[44] Munford's financial and legal talents were helpful also in the establishment of Courts of Assize and a Board of Trade. On 20 October, he was appointed to the committee directed to prepare a bill "for establishing Courts of Assize," where he worked with John Taylor, Mason, Tyler, and Henry. Though not named chairman, on 6 December Munford reported for the Committee of the Whole the amendments made to the bill.[45] On 5 November he was added to the committee to amend the act establishing the Board of Trade.[46]

But Munford's most important services in the fall, 1779 session concerned military affairs. In the previous session he had worked on the committee which was trying to set up a munitions plant at Westham. Now, on 6 November, he was named on a committee to evaluate the management of the gun manufactory at Fredericksburg, and on 12 November he reported for this committee.[47] On 27 October he was recognized as the leader in military preparedness. He was appointed chairman of the committee, including Henry, "for more effectually providing against invasions and insurrections." The bill of that committee was presented by Munford on 3 November; but it was then shelved for more comprehensive legislation.[48] Munford then headed several committees which prepared the comprehensive legislation of 2 December 1779.

On 30 November Munford reported for the committee of the Whole concerning the state of the Commonwealth. He recommended fifteen resolutions. These covered a wide range of military matters in both the army and the navy. The principal resolutions affecting the army did not suggest any reduction except in the number of officers. Only one regiment was to be stationed on the Western frontier, and the number of infantry corps and regiments should be reduced, but each regiment was to be brought up to full strength. The effect should have been to provide greater strength in army, cavalry, artillery, and the state garrison regiment. Recommendations for the navy, on the other hand, called for a reduction in the number of ships and specified the vessels to be sold or released. The only improvement was the suggestion of better regulations for the conduct of sailors.[49] To prepare bills pursuant to these resolutions Munford headed two committees. Two days later, on 2 December 1779, he presented several bills representing their work. His bills "to regulate and ascertain the number of land forces to be kept up for the defense of the State" were passed by the House and approved later in the month. The act incorporating them satisfied the fifteen original resolutions but included also a cessation of enlistments as of 1 February 1780.[50]

The prologue of the act reveals as much concern for economy as for military preparedness: "THAT the state may incur no greater expense than the exegencies of affairs requires, and that the publick revenue may be aided by every means which prudence and economy dictate. . . ."[51] The whole act was prepared by a legislature more immediately concerned with inflation than with an invasion. Few had seen an invasion first-hand; all had felt keenly the effects of inflation. Moreover the restoration of a balanced economy was indeed a serious concern for Virginia, and Virginians were not aware that war was soon to be brought home to them. But Virginia was negligent as well as shortsighted: it had not met its quota in supplying troops for the Continental army, and the legislature was now providing for its own cavalry and artillery at the expense of forces earmarked previously for the Eastern service.

Munford was not alone to blame for Virginia's lack of preparedness when invasion actually came. Nor was Thomas Jefferson, who was popularly made the scapegoat. Nor was the Ways and Means Committee, although the tone of economy was apparent in a report made by that committee on 27 November, several days before Munford submitted his bills: "The deranged state of the army, and the ruinous situation of the navy, hath greatly enhanced the expense of maintaining the one, & subtracted from that little defence which was expected to be derived from the other; whilst the accumulated charge of both, creates an article of expenditure which hath already reduced your finances to difficulty, and is too enormous to be supported."[52] This attitude toward the need for economy characterized the whole of Virginia, where many voices were raised later in recrimination.

His important legislative responsibilities, however, were not Munford's sole concern. For several years his daughters, Elizabeth and Ursula Anna, had doubtless made extended visits to the homes of friends and relatives in the manner fashionable among Virginia families living on widely separated plantations. These visits were probably promoted by the mother and encouraged or at least approved by the father and became more frequent as the girls approached marriageable age. In July, 1778, for example, Elizabeth was visiting Mrs. Elizabeth H. Farley at Nesting, just across the river from Mrs. Randolph, a Munford cousin.[53] It was doubtless here at Nesting that Ursula was to meet her future husband, Mrs. Farley's brother Francis Otway Byrd.

But Elizabeth was the elder, the first to make such visits, and the first to be married. On 26 April 1780 she reached the age of eighteen; on 16 May Richard Kennon signed a marriage bond and they were married perhaps that very day.[54] Kennon was the

son of Robert Kennon of Mt. Pleasant, in Chesterfield County, and
Sara Skipwith Kennon, sister of Sir Peyton. Richard Kennon
had entered the Revolutionary army as a lieutenant in the Fifth
Virginia Regiment and was destined to become a brigadier general of state militia, in 1789 to take his father-in-law's place as
County Lieutenant of Mecklenburg County, and ultimately, in
1801, to become Speaker of the Virginia Senate.[55] Concerning the
wedding festivities the only records which have survived are a
scatalogical poem by St. George Tucker and the outraged protest
of the Grand Jury, which on 8 May returned Tucker for "pro-
fanely swearing four oaths at Colonel Munford's Fishery." The
wedding festivities were thus quite prolonged and, as Tucker's
poem makes clear, "Guests were plentier far than bedding." Some
house guests, like George and Edward Tarry, lived just across
the Roanoke River; others, like Carter Littlepage and Tucker,
came from some distance.[56]

When Munford returned to the House of Delegates in May,
1780, he was given a few, relatively trivial duties. The most important was his appointment on 8 June as one of the committee
"to embody five thousand men, for the defense of this and our
sister States."[57] He evidently left soon afterwards. Probably discussion in this committee and general talk among the delegates
tended to make him feel responsible for the general state of
unpreparedness which followed the laws which he had written and
seen through the last session of the House. For on 12 May General
Lincoln had surrendered at Charleston, South Carolina, and half
the Continentals imprisoned were Virginians. The shock felt in
Virginia was a sudden reawakening. And it was perhaps tempting to
hold responsible a man who remained at home supervising his
daughter's wedding instead of fulfilling his duties in the House.

Whether or not Munford felt partly responsible, he displayed
a public spirited generosity in his attempts to relieve the needs
of the captured men. For their relief he expended considerable
effort and money. Soon after the surrender he and Thomas Person,
of North Carolina, signed a letter of credit on behalf of General
Scott and the others for £500 or more.[58] But petitions by Person
and Munford to export tobacco to cover this expense were
unavailing. As late as 31 December 1781, Munford was writing
General Greene concerning this difficulty: "My principal Motive
for troubling you with this Letter is, to beg the Favour of you,
if you can, to inform a Gentleman of the name of Colcock in
Charles Town, that I would have remitted to him the Money or the
Value thereof, which he upon my Note obligingly advanced to

some Officers in Captivity at Hudrel's point. I have applyed to the Executive of two States for permission to export Tobacco. From some political Reason, I doubt not, I have been refused. I have ever been happy to hear of my General's Safety, and God bless you."[59] It was probably to make arrangement concerning the relief of these prisoners that Munford had entertained Governor John Rutledge of South Carolina at Richland earlier that year.[60]

Before Munford returned to the House of Delegates on 25 October 1780, America suffered its worst defeat of the war, at Camden, South Carolina, on 16 August. And the Virginia militia played the most ignominious role in this worst defeat. When they faced the charging British troops they turned, threw away their muskets, and ran. Their own general, Edward Stevens, reported to Thomas Jefferson: ". . . with respect to the Militia themselves, it matters not, for from their Rascally Behaviour they deserve no pity. Their Cowardly Behaviour has indeed given a Mortal Wound to my Feelings. I expect that near one half of the Militia will never halt till they get Home. And from what I have already seen I think I may venture to say that out of those who may be Collected, there will not be more than one fourth of them that will have their Arms, many of them you [may] depend have thrown away their Arms with an expectation of getting Home by it."[61]

Humiliated by news of the defeat at Camden, esecially by the wild flight of the Virginia militia, Munford as commanding officer of the Mecklenburg militia took disciplinary measures which he was required to take. On 28 August he wrote to General Gates:

I have ordered twelve of my Militia under the Command of Capt. Lt. Scott as a Guard to the Waggon sent on with Ammunition and Stores from the Magazine in this County, to Hillsbrough. As soon as I was informed of the unlucky Affair near Camden, I ordered Detachments of my Militia to patrole and guard the several passes upon Roanoke River, to intercept any Militia or Regulars who might attempt to cross without permits from their commanding Officers. In Consequence of this Measure, several Delinquents have been apprehended. Capt. Lt. Scott will deliver twelve of these Miscreants, and I shall in a few Days send on a larger Number of these Gentry. I should be happy upon any Occasion to lend my assistance to the Operations of the Army under your Command. . . .[62]

About two weeks later, on 14 September, he wrote again to Gates: "I have sent under the Command of Cap'n Walker Seventy of the Militia who were of Gen'l Stephens' Brigade. I have furnished the Guard with Eight Muskets from the Magazine at this station. There are now remaining about thirty of the Militia, apprehended by my order, who are on Furloe, being sick. I shall continue to take up, and send on, any of this flying Corps who may fall into my hands, untill you will be pleased to communicate to me upon this subject."[63]

Munford was not returning these men for summary punishment; he was returning them to duty, and those who had fled from the field of battle did not need to fear the consequences of the recent, severe legislation concerning desertion. These provisions were to take effect forty days after the end of the assembly and were obviously not in operation until 21 August, several days after the battle.[64] But troops continued to desert. On 21 August, Stevens wrote to General Gates that he had "Officers ahead to stop all of the Virginia Militia from going home."[65] On 30 August he wrote to Thomas Jefferson, ". . . by the Inclosed return you'll see the whole Militia, Great Desertions has taken place. This has been in consequence of their being Armed and ordered forward again and this fully proves they never had any intention of rendering their Country Service. Judge what my Situation must be. My Pen cannot describe the trouble and Feelings I have had since I first took Charge of them. Such disgracefull behaviour I believe was never Instanced before."[66]

The day before Munford returned to the House of Delegates, in Richmond, General Mordecai Gist, who had been given the task of recruiting and supplying the Southern Army, wrote to him from Baltimore. Gist had distinguished himself for gallantry at Camden and had evidently stopped at Richland on his way north. Munford had kept his horse for him,[67] and Gist requested his compliments to "the Ladies of your family." But the letter was not a personal one. Gist was writing to the man who in a previous session had guided bills on military preparedness. He was writing a well reasoned letter calculated to shame Munford into doing what he could to urge the legislature into full effort on behalf of the nation. Gist was quite dissatisfied with the Virginia period of an eighteen-month enlistment, with the bounty system of recruiting, and with other faults in which Munford was more especially guilty: "This with the manifest neglect to fill up your quota of Troops in the Continental Army, and to protect the trade in Chesapeake, was impolitic in itself, if not criminally injurious to the Union. . . .

". . . Pardon me my Dear sir if my Candor calls the blush to your Cheek; your Integrity is above the reach of Censure, & I have that confidence in your abilities, which inclines me to hope, when joined with the influence of other good members of your Assembly, that the present Sessions will terminate to the Honor of Virginia."[68]

The letter may indeed have shamed Munford, but he had lost any power which he had possessed earlier towards effecting these reforms. His reception at the House of Delegates on 25 October 1780 was cool indeed. He was not, as in previous sessions, named to the Committees of Propositions and Grievances or Privileges and Elections. He was appointed, on 10 November, to the money committee; and on 4 December he headed the routine committee to examine the enrolled bills.[69] But he seems to have become inactive shortly afterwards. He had probably departed, for on 23 December the Sergeant of Arms was instructed to take into custody the delegates from Mecklenburg, Goode and Munford, both of whom were absent without permission.[70] Perhaps Munford could no longer endure the treatment which he felt that he was receiving as the scapegoat of unpreparedness, especially after the inglorious flight at Camden reflected upon his training of the Southside militia. Doubtless his own repressed sense of responsibility gnawed at him, and at his enforced inactivity he grew restless. Moreover, although he did not ask to be excused, he was needed elsewhere. The military situation in Southside Virginia was becoming alarming, and he was needed there both as County Lieutenant of Mecklenburg County and as Quartermaster at Taylor's Ferry.

A major difficulty for regulars and militia alike at Camden and later at Guildford Court House was the problem of procuring arms, ammunition, and food. On 1 August 1780, for example, General Stevens wrote General Gates complaining of his soldiers' lack of food; and on 28 January 1781, General Lawson, writing to Governor Jefferson from McKee's Mills, North Carolina, complained that they lacked shelter and supplies; there were no tents, and no axes to cut firewood for the men, who were dropping off because of illness.[71] In alleviating these difficulties Munford was especially helpful during the period from 1780 until 1782, for he was instrumental in building up, often by raiding his own plantation, a regular commissary at Banks Old Stone, half a mile from Taylor's Ferry, where he acted as Quartermaster.[72] Here he provided for the men meal, flour, bacon, pork, beef, and fish; and for their horses, corn, oats, and fodder. A blacksmith, perhaps Munford's Wheelwright Billy, was on hand to shoe horses, and occasionally Munford was able to procure a horse or mare for army use.[73] As early as 15 December 1780 this supply depot and magazine was the subject of a local complaint lodged by Bennett Goode: "The three months the last Guard had to serve at the Magazine at Taylors Ferry is Expired. With difficulty we have furnished a temporary guard to serve untill your Excellency Order in what manner a standing guard be furnished. The difficulty of furnishing a guard arises from the abuses committed on the soldiers by Continental Officers when at that Station. Col. Edward Carrington caned a serjent and Ordered two of the soldiars striped and whiped which was Executed with out the formality of a trial."[74] Since Colonel Carrington had just written General Gates to recommend Richland as a stopping point on his way north,[75] Munford himself had evidently not remonstrated with Carrington, then in command. The depot was maintained until after the surrender of Cornwallis.[76]

On 2 January 1781 Jefferson alerted all Southside county lieutenants of the approaching enemy; and on 13 January he requested 212 militia from Mecklenburg County.[77] For a while there was some uncertainty concerning the enemy's intentions. When it became apparent that a thrust north towards Virginia was planned, the Southside militia were called out. Before 12 February Munford was promoted from his position at the head of the Mecklenburg militia to command the militia of three counties, Mecklenburg, Lunenburg, and Brunswick. Since the militia from these three counties had for some time constituted a unified training group with a parade ground in Mecklenburg County and since Munford evidently had seniority over the other county lieutenants, his elevation to this command was to be expected. He accepted it and began preparations to embody his militia and equip them to take the field when ordered to do so.

When Munford was appointed by General Lawson to command the militia of three Southside counties, Lewis Burwell assumed Munford's former duties as county lieutenant of Mecklenburg County.[78] Burwell was given separate instructions by General Greene on 17 February 1781:

> You will engage as many of the Militia as you can Arm and equip properly to serve with the Army for six weeks, unless circumstances should render it convenient to discharge them sooner. Embody none that are not possessed of good sound constitutions and capable of enduring Hardships, and that can furnish their own Arms as we have none. . . .
> You will march your men when collected up to the mouth of the Stanton River and let the men bring into the field with them eight or ten days provision. The Militia must come as lightly equipt as possible, as no baggage is, or can be with the Army. . . .
> The moment you have collected your force you will advertise me of your numbers and condition.—[79]

Evidently Burwell took charge with more enthusiasm than discretion. On 25 February General Lawson wrote to Jefferson that he had ordered out the militia of Prince Edward, Cumberland, Amelia, Charlotte, Lunenburg, Mecklenburg, Brunswick, Buckingham, and Amhurst counties.[80] Disobeying instructions about the tour of duty for which he was to embody his men, Burwell drew them out for three months, marched them towards North Carolina, and then abandoned them in camp. The story is told by Burwell in his pettish complaint to General Greene:

> The second day after I left Camp I meet the Mecklenburg Militia in their own County headed by Colonel Munford and upon enquire found they had been stoped by his orders and carried back to Taylors Ferry. The Men when ordered out by me were drawn out agreeable to their divisions and subject by Law to a Tour of three Months if their Services were required so long and in Case of desertion were liable to be made Regulars for 8 Months but Colonel Munford has by General Lawsons instructions (from whom he derives his authority) drawn them out as Volunteers for six Weeks which puts it out of our power to punish them in the County should they return without leave.
>
> I intended to have returned to Camp and made an offer of my Services provided I could have had my rank but my horse was taken so lame and ill that after waiting a day with him on the road I was obliged to turn homewards and was much puzzled to get there. Enclosed is a Commission sent me by General Lawson which I can by no means accept while I have the honour to command a County but more especially when Gentlemen that have not seen Service and hold no Commissions in the Militia are put over the heads of the Militia Officers[.] General Lawson is a Man of Sensibility and would I am sure in the like circumstances be one of the first to remonstrate against such proceedings[.] I have always been ready to expose my Person in defence of my Country and am still so if your Excellency chuses to give me command but must say I was much mortified at having the Command of our Men taken from me and given to another.[81]

Meanwhile, as has been seen, Munford had assumed charge. On 24 February, writing to General Greene from Taylor's Ferry, he reported his progress in carrying out orders and requested some directions:

> In Obedience to the Orders I have received from Brigadier General Lawson, I am collecting with the greatest Dispatch two Battalions of Militia from the Counties of Lunenburg Mecklenburg and Brunswick which the General has commissioned me with the Command of, and directed me to march to your Army as soon as they can be arranged and furnished with Arms.
>
> I doubt not but I shall execute these Orders in a few Days, and

that I shall be happy enough to join you with a chosen Corps. The Arms are not so well calculated for Service as I could wish. I shall be glad to receive your Orders in bringing up these Men, as I am a Stranger to your present Fashion.[82]

After correcting Burwell's disobedience, which seems to have been calculated to make the penalty for desertion less frightening, Munford was on 1 March ordered to Hillsborough by General Greene's aid-de-camp, Nathaniel Pendleton.[83] He left at once. On 2 March St. George Tucker wrote to his wife: ". . . we are two Miles beyond Roanoke having cross'd at Taylors Ferry last Night— that we know nothing certain either of the Enemy or Genl. Green except that the latter will probably be ten thousand strong in a few Days—allow one half for Lies & he will still have a pretty considerable Army—400. Men under Coll Munford 400. Regulars from Chest. C. House, & 300 with us make above one thousand of the number."[84] On 3 March, Munford informed General Greene that he had reached camp about thirteen miles from Hugh Dobbin's.[85] On the following day he wrote anxiously,

Agreeable to your's I have wheeled my Regiment off towards Hillsborough and this Day we have marched twelve Miles, advanced towards that place.

For want of a few Horse I am much at a Loss, the Difficulty of procuring Scouts in this horrid Country, and the Impossibility of impressing a single Horse for their Use renders my Situation disagreeable.

We want Flints, loose Powder and Buckshot or Cartridges. I shall proceed however in my Rout agreeable to the Latitude you have given, provided I have no express Orders. Pray my dear General send off to me immediately.

I am very Ill myself with the Gout, which has taken me since I left home. I have not a Field Officer with me.[86]

He received permission to return home; but despite his gout he was by 10 March back at Taylor's Ferry acting as Quartermaster. When conflict became imminent, however, Munford returned to camp despite his illness and played his part in the battle of Guildford Court House. There he yielded to Colonel Henry Skipwith, younger brother of Sir Peyton and an experienced officer, command of the regiment with which he had been commissioned and evidently commanded instead the Mecklenburg militia in the absence of its colonel, Burwell. The action is fully and vividly described by St. George Tucker in a letter to his wife, Munford's first cousin, a letter which Munford himself carried north:

You may perhaps expect that I can give you some account of the Battle. I must candidly acknowledge myself totally incapable of doing so. I will only tell you that Lawson's Brigade composed a Line near the center of which my post was. A Cannonade of half an hour usher'd in the Battle. Our Friend Skipwith was posted in the express direction of the shot, and with his Batallion maintain'd his post during a most tremendous Fire with a firmness that does him much honor. Coll. Holcome's Regt. was on the Right of him, and on my Left, so that I was in perfect security during the wholetime except from a few shot which came in the Direction towards me. Beverley was still further on the right. When the Cannonade ceased orders were given for Holcome's Regt. and the other Regt. on the right of him to advance and annoy the Enemy's left Flank. While we were advancing to execute these Orders, the British had advanced and having turned the Flank of Coll. Munford's Regt. in which Skipwith Commanded as Major, we discover'd them in our rear: This threw the Militia into such confusion that without attending in the least to their Officers who endeavoured to halt them and make them face about and engage the Enemy Holcome's Regiment and ours instantly broke off without firing a single Gun and dispers'd like a Flock of sheep frighted by Dogs. With infinite Labour Beverley and myself rallied about sixty or seventy of our Men and brought them to the charge. Holcome was not so successful. He could not rally a Man tho. assisted by John Woodson who acted very gallantly. With the few Men which he had collected we at several different times maintained an irregular kind of skirmishing with the British and were once successful enough to drive a party for a very small distance. On the Ground we past over I think I saw about eight or ten Men killed and wounded. The greatest satisfaction I had during the Battle was in riding over one of the haughty British officers who was lying prostrate at the Root of a Tree, genteely dress'd. One of our soldiers gave him a dram as he was expiring and bade him die like a brave man. How different this conduct from that of the Barbarians he had commanded!

In attempting to rally a party of regular Troops I received a Wound in the small of my Leg from a soldier, who either from design or accident held his Bayonet in such a direction that I could not possibly avoid it as I rode up to stop him from running away. The Bay'net penetrated about an Inch and a half between the Bones of my Leg. I felt no Inconvenience from it for some hours, but have since been obliged to hobble with the Assistance of a stick or of some person to lead me. After this our Militia join'd the Virginia Regulars under Coll. Campbell and sustain a good smart fire for some Minutes. We were soon after ordered to retreat. Whilst we were doing so, Tarleton advanced to attack us with his horse, but a party of continentals who were fortunately close behind us gave him so warm a

Reception that he retreated with some Degree of Precipitation. A few Minutes after we halted by the side of an old Field Fence and observ'd him with his Legion surveying us at the distance of two or three hundred yards. He did not think proper to attack us again as we were advantageously posted and the continentals who had encountered him just before were still in our rear. After this the whole Army retreated in good order to the Iron Works fifteen Miles from the Field of Battle, having lost the Field and our Artillery—but how these things happened I cannot tell, for during the whole of the Battle I knew nothing of what pass'd in any other Quarter than on the ground where our Regiment was engaged. . . .

. . . Major Hubbard of Coll. Munford's Regt. had the Skirt of his surtout Coat shot away by a Cannon Ball and his horse slightly wounded by the same. There were not, however, above ten men kill'd and wounded during the whole Cannonade in which I believe six pieces of Artillery were constantly employ'd for half an hour.

Beverley sustained no other Injury during the action than the Loss of his Blankets, which were on his horse. He was too intent upon the Business in hand to discover the Loss till the Battle was over. Lawson, Skipwith, Munford, Holcome, and every other officer of your Acquaintance sustaind none at all.[87]

The casualty lists speak eloquently for the heroism of the Virginia militia; and Munford, disregarding his illness and surrendering his command to one more experienced, showed himself a courageous and unselfish patriot. Still ailing, he was again given permission to return home. On 2 April he wrote to General Greene from Richland, "I am much obliged to you for your Permit to return Home. I am now so far recovered from my Indisposition, that I can again attend your Commands, and it will make me happy to exicute your Orders."[88]

With the battle of Guildford Court House ended Munford's brief career as an American soldier. But he continued to act as Quartermaster procuring food and materials. He also continued his correspondence with General Greene on various matters. On 3 April 1781 he sent a note with Mr. William Colbreath, father of a soldier formerly belonging to Munford's regiment, requesting Greene's efforts to secure the son's exchange "if you can, consistently, procure" it.[89] On 13 July, still suffering from gout, he wrote to apprize Greene, "I fear from the Accounts I receive, the Enemy may approach nearer me, and that dayly."[90] On 12 July he sent to Greene the son of Major Carlisle, perhaps asking for verbal instructions: "I make no Doubt you will act by him, as I will to any person you do me the Honour to recommend."[91] Meanwhile Lewis Burwell had again assumed command of the

Mecklenburg militia and would redeem himself by leading them in the Yorktown campaign.[92]

During the year Munford gave his younger daughter, Ursula Anna, in marriage to Otway Byrd.[93] Francis Otway Byrd, the son of William Byrd III and Elizabeth Carter Byrd, had become an officer in the British navy and was serving aboard the *Fowey* when Munford and the other burgesses came aboard to negotiate with Governor Dunmore. Although his father's will cut him off with a shilling if he left the navy without his step-mother's permission, by 6 May 1776 he was acting as an aid-de-camp to General Charles Lee at Williamsburg; and when Lee proceeded south to Charleston, they evidently visited the reconciled father at Westover on route. At Sullivan's Island, South Carolina, Otway Byrd performed his duty with especial courage, and General Lee remembered him affectionately in his will. By January of 1777 Byrd had been commissioned Lieutenant Colonel of the Third Virginia Light Dragoons.[94] Munford provided generously for his daughter, causing Mrs. Elizabeth Farley to comment that her brother Otway's bride had brought him "a clever little Fortune." "She is an amiable little Girl," she added "& makes our Brother happy."[95]

About the same time Munford made provision also for a nephew, William Beverley Fitzhugh, the son of his sister-in-law Ursula Beverley Fitzhugh and Colonel William Fitzhugh.[96] The father, who evidently had tory leanings, left only the legally re-quired shilling to his eldest son, Robert Fitzhugh, if he should return to the state, because he left home at the beginning of the war and failed to correspond with his father. To William Beverley Fitzhugh the father left only two Negroes, probably personal servants,[97] though he was one of the wealthiest men in the state, with 345 slaves.[98]

Having resigned his duties as County Lieutenant, seen his daughters married, and probably suffering increasingly with gout, Munford evidently took to drink, as his father before him had done during his last years. On 11 May 1782, Colonel Burwell, writing to Colonel Davies, charged, ". . . the Senior Acting Magis-trate (Col: Munford) *had so given himself up to drink, that he was not capable of attending to business.* . . ."[99] Two days later Munford was returned by the grand jury "for profane swearing one Oath," and his fine he duly paid rather than have the case come to trial.[100]

The next year, 1783, saw Munford's final decline and death. On 10 March 1783 the magistrates of Mecklenburg County adopted a singular remonstrance:

Ordered that the Clerk wait upon his excellency the Governor & council with the Humble address and remonstrance of the Court representing to them that the worthy and Judicious conduct of Col. Robert Munford one of their Members, they have long considered as a peculiar happiness to this County and it is with sorrow and regret that they must now complain of him, from the excess of Drink & Intoxication not only neglecting the duties of a Magistrate, but frequently by his indecent and disorderly behaviour interrupting the business of the Court in such a manner as to render it impossible for the Court to proceed in their necessary duty—The Court therefore prays that his excellency with advice of Council will renew the Commission of peace for this county leaving out the name of the said Robert Munford.[101]

Such a remonstrance could have been provoked only by conduct indeed unbecoming for the Virginia gentleman Munford had hitherto shown himself to be, and would seem to indicate an utter lack of concern. But he could not allow the scandal to become publicized. On 15 April 1783 he resigned his seat as a gentleman justice of Mecklenburg; and on that same day it was "Ordered that the remonstrance to the Governor and Council respecting the Conduct of Robert Munford be rescinded."[102] On 13 May, Henry Deloney dropped a suit against Munford, but several suits were instituted against him for debt, the last on 10 December 1783.[103] By 1 June 1783 his family evidently gave up all hope of his recovery. Writing to Robert McKenzie, Robert Beverley commented, ". . . our friend M—d has given in to an habit of the most uncommon intemperance—so much so that there can be no hopes of reclaiming him—your handsome mention of my sister I shall not fail to communicate to her—it will be some comfort to her in her present unhappy situation—"[104] On 16 December he made his will, and before the end of the year, he was dead.[105]

His will was proved 8 February 1784. His daughters had already been provided for, and their dowries the will merely confirmed. To his wife he left the use of his Richland plantation during the rest of her life, a third of the profit from the estate, also the household servants, the post chaise and horses, the silver plate, and the household furniture. The rest of the estate went to his son, William.[106]

He was buried on his Richland plantation, near the present shore of the Roanoke River, now swollen by the Buggs Island Dam, beneath a gravestone from which time has obliterated all charactery. His widow remained at Richland, its glories gradually fading. In his diary for 15 May 1792 Richard N. Venable recorded a visit there: ". . . to Charles Kennon's, a kind hospitable man who married Robert Munford's daughter, and now lives where Munford formerly did. I take a view of the improvements made by Munford, all of which have the appearance of magnificence, but alas how changed! I see also Mrs. Munford who gives us a family history, but these republican days have defaced it much."[107] After the death of Anna Munford in September, 1803, William sold Richland in 1809.[108] Already dilapidated, it gradually disintegrated and was finally consumed by fire.

Although these monuments did not endure, his progeny and his plays have survived to honor "Virginia's first and only comic son." His daughter Ursula evidently never published her novel.[109] But before the end of the century his son exhibited his fondness for his father's memory by editing Munford's literary works and became distinguished in his own right in both the fields in which his father had been eminent—literature and government. In 1798 William Munford published his miscellany, *Poems and Compositions in Prose on Several Occasions*, including a drama; and in 1846, two decades after his death, his translation of *The Iliad* was published. After his legal studies with George Wythe, his political rise was steady. From 1797 to 1802 he served in the House of Delegates; from 1802 until 1806 in the Senate; from 1806 until 1811 on the Council of State; and from 1811 until his death, as Clerk of the House. Most of his works he actually produced in connection with his duties there. He collaborated with William Walter Hening in editing the Virginia *Reports* until Hening died; then he undertook sole editorial responsibilities. William's son George Wythe Munford was similarly distinguished in literature and politics. The accomplishments of Robert Munford's progeny were many, but his plays, *The Candidates* and *The Patriots*, were his main legacy.

V

Dramatist: *The Candidates*

For the writing of his plays, Munford had of course no native models whatever to assist him. The few awkward efforts to the north in tragedy, comic opera, and farce had certainly established no foundation for native drama. Perforce Munford relied instead upon English models for his plots and techniques. These models he could have found in his own library or perhaps in the volumes borrowed from the library of William Byrd III, which was especially rich in dramatic literature.[1] He doubtless also remembered the plays which, as a schoolboy, he had enjoyed in the company or at the expense of his uncle Beverley.

But the most apt models were the comedies and farces he had seen performed at Williamsburg, Petersburg, and Hobb's Hole. From about the time he completed his legal studies in Williamsburg, Virginia was one of the three theatrical centers in Colonial America, and Williamsburg was certainly the dramatic capital there. David Douglass' London Company spent its first season in Virginia from October of 1760 until May of 1761, and returned for performances in 1762 and 1763. Then in 1767 William Verling organized his Virginia Company in Norfolk and during the spring of 1768 played in Williamsburg. About two years later, in June of 1770, Douglass' American Company played in Virginia for the greater part of eighteen months, making its major stays in the capital.[2] Munford probably witnessed the arrival of the group, for he was in Williamsburg that June; and, like George Washington, he doubtless arranged to attend performances whenever he could—in Williamsburg during sessions of the House of Burgesses or the General Court, in Hobb's Hole whenever he was visiting the Beverleys or the Mills, and in Petersburg while he was visiting his Mother or other nearby relatives. Quite possibly he planned, or even wrote his *Candidates* for one of these performances. Thus the plays of Munford are English in their plotting and techniques and to some extent in their characterizations. But *The Candidates* and *The Patriots* are not slavish imitations of English plays; instead, they utilize traditional techniques to dramatize basically native characters and themes.

The first proper American farce was Munford's *The Candidates; or, the Humors of a Virginia Election.* Though designated upon its title page as a comedy, it was more accurately classified by William Munford, in a letter of 1792, as a farce.[3] It lacks the traditional five acts and the romance of the proper, full-length comedy and was probably intended to serve as the lighter after-piece in the traditional eighteenth century dramatic double bill demanded in Williamsburg just as much as in London. It was first published by his son, William, in 1798.[4] The prologue, "By a Friend," was probably written by William to accompany publication. The first recorded performance of the play came on 18-19 January 1949, when it was successfully acted at the William and Mary Theater in Williamsburg.[5] Although it is usually dated about 1770, the year of composition seems quite uncertain. The earliest possible date is the winter of 1770-1771; the setting of the play is the election following the death of Governor Botetourt on 15 October 1770, and none of the references in the play seem to postdate that year. They are quite consistently references to Virginia, especially Southside Virginia, affairs in the late 1760's. But the play could have been written at any time during the decade; and Munford may well have written it in the late 1770's as an afterpiece for *The Patriots.* It is quite unlikely that it was written after 1780.

In *The Candidates* Munford dramatized the mutual responsibilities of voter and delegate in a system of representative democracy: the responsibility of the voter to elect the best qualified candidate and the obligation of the able, qualified gentleman to accept and even campaign for public office. More specifically, *The Candidates* dramatizes the election of delegates to the Virginia House of Burgesses. The hero, Wou'dbe, an able and disinterested gentleman who has for years served his country as burgess, finds his own re-election uncertain; and his perennial colleague, Worthy, has decided to retire from politics. The other candidates are all quite objectionable: Sir John Toddy is a toper; Mr. Strutabout, a cox-comb; and Mr. Smallhopes, a "jockey." From the very start the campaign managers of these candidates circulate damaging rumors. They allege that Mr. Wou'dbe has caused the recent increase in taxes and that he insists upon Sir John as a running mate. In campaign style familiar to the South ever since, the other candidates promise that they will accomplish all that the freeholders wish. Mr. Wou'dbe, on the other hand, refuses to commit himself on proposals which in his judgment are uncertain or undesirable. The voters are understandably confused. Just before the poll, however, Worthy reconsiders and declares himself again a candidate. His criticism of the opposition and support of Wou'dbe assure success for both.

Although the political plot is serious and devoid of romantic interest, slapstick and farce provide comic relief, furnished mainly by the Guzzles. In the first act John Guzzle, campaign manager for Sir John Toddy, visits Wou'dbe with an empty bottle. Already tipsy, he soon hints:

. . . my bottle never was so long a filling in this house, before; surely, there's a leak in the bottom, (*looks at it again*).
Wou'dbe. What have you got in your bottle, John, a lizard?
Guzzle. Yes, a very uncommon one, and I want a little rum put to it, to preserve it.
Wou'dbe. Hav'n't you one in your belly, John?
Guzzle. A dozen, I believe, by their twisting, when I mentioned the rum.
Wou'dbe. Would you have rum to preserve them, too? (pp. 23-24)

In Act II, at a pre-election barbecue Joan Guzzle drinks so much that she loses consciousness. John circulates among the crowd with amusing drunken dialogue and with huzzas until Sir John too "reclines." Guzzle places Joan beside the recumbent knight. When, sobering up, she finds Sir John lying beside her and her husband apparently suspicious, she begins to beat the knight in exasperation and berates him with a typical Restoration reproach: "I'll learn you to cuckold a man without letting his wife know it" (p. 40).

In both of his plays Munford gave type names to most of his characters, in the traditional fashion of English satiric comedy. He was aiming at a general, a universal effect. But sometimes in *The Candidates*, as often in *The Patriots*, he had in mind prominent Southside originals. The prologue seems to draw attention to both the personal satire and the universality of the play:

> Here characters, whose names are now unknown,
> Shall shine again, as in their spheres they shone;
> While some may make malicious explanation,
> And know them all still living in the nation. (p. xi)

One rare example of undisguised personal satire appears early in the play when Ralpho introduces Guzzle: "Master, rare news, here's our neighbor Guzzle, as drunk as ever Chief Justice Cornelius was upon the bench" (p. 21). Cornelius Carghill was senior magistrate of Lunenburg County when Munford first sat with a county commission, but his drunkenness must have been proverbial. In May, 1761 the Lunenburg Grand Jury, its patience exhausted, returned him for "Profane Swearing four Oaths and getting Drunk."[6]

Of the two successful candidates, Wou'dbe, whose name was possibly suggested by the two Wou'dbees of Farquhar's popular *Twin Rivals*, seems in certain aspects to be possibly an idealized picture of Munford himself, who was actually elected in 1770, as in previous years, along with his colleague Matthew Marrable. In one passage at least the dramatist seems autobiographical. After serving his breakfast guests with some "fine salt shad," Wou'dbe is queried:

> *Prize.* Mr. Wou'dbe, do your fishing places succeed well this year?
> *Wou'dbe.* Better than they've been known for some seasons.
> *Stern.* I'm very glad of it: for then I can get my supply from you.
> (p. 47)

In 1769, the year before that in which the play is set, Munford invested heavily in a fishery on Cow Island.[7] These fisheries were later to play a part in feeding Virginia soldiers during the Revolution.[8] In the selection of campaign promises and issues, too, as will be seen later, Munford was treating his own recent political experience with lighthearted irony.

The other successful candidate, the retired and reluctant Worthy, perhaps derives his name from Mrs. Susanna Centlivre's *Gotham Election* (1715), or from Farquhar's *Recruiting Officer*, if indeed such a popular type name demands a source. But the original of the character is more difficult to ascertain. Munford's actual colleague in 1769 and 1770 was Matthew Marrable, whose considerable property in Mecklenburg and Charlotte counties adjoined Munford's Finneywood property. A well-to-do planter, merchant, and ordinary-keeper, with a tavern in Williamsburg as well as in Mecklenburg County, Marrable had in the House of Burgesses represented Lunenburg and Mecklenburg counties; and in April of 1765 he became a member of the commission for Charlotte County.[9] He was quite irascible, and he and Munford frequently quarreled. On 10 March 1772 Marrable refused to permit their joint property lines to be processioned.[10] On 15 September 1778 he instituted against Munford a lawsuit, the nature of which has not been ascertained, but which was on 9 November

1778 certified, along with six other Marrable suits, to the General Court.[11] Munford responded by publishing in the Virginia *Gazette* for 21 August 1779 a poem addressed to "M———M———— of Meck————g," as written by the Devil to a favorite son; he wrote several others similarly directed but evidently first published by his son.[12] Thus Marrable was hardly the exact prototype of Worthy. But although Marrable was evidently a man of violent passions, he and Munford probably got along well enough generally, for Elizabeth Munford remembered garrulous correspondence from Marrable to the family. "P. S.," she added in a letter of 1815, "And a long one it will be, as old Nat. [sic] Marable once said, when he wrote a postscript containing eleven pages."[13] Interestingly enough, on 1 June 1771 Marrable was suing John Speed, Jr.,[14] who may have been the model for the unsuccessful Strutabout of the play. Despite the fact, then, that Marrable was actually Munford's successful colleague in the election, Munford is not likely to have cast him in the role of Worthy, who is rather the type of modest, retiring, public-spirited Virginia burgess.

The unsuccessful candidates also seem primarily general types rather than attempts to ridicule any particular local politicians. For example, Sir John Toddy seems basically a typical English stage country squire, a late and pale Sir John Falstaff. But his title immediately suggests a possible original in Sir Peyton Skipwith, the local baronet. Later, in *The Patriots*, Sir Peyton seems to have been cast for the role of the turncoat Tackabout. Munford particularizes the contest as that of 1770, and Worthy identifies the other candidates as their opponents in the previous election also, but these defeated candidates would be recognized only locally. They seem instead to be popular Virginia types. Of the two "Jackanapes" Wou'dbe deplores the time "when coxcombs and jockies can impose themselves upon it [the county] for men of learning" (p. 35). And Captain Paunch remarks, "Mr. Strutabout would do very well if he was not such a coxcomb. As for Smallhopes, I'd as soon send to New-Market, for a burgess, as send him . . ." (p. 19). The New Market Captain Paunch mentions was not only the popular English racing center, but was probably also the plantation of John Baylor of Caroline, where the famous "Fearnought" was at stud.

For his "jockey" Munford may have been satirizing one of the Goodes. "Racehorse" John Goode owned an impressive list of famous quarterhorse racers, some of which brought him fortunes on the racing paths. He purchased the renowned "Janus," the sire of many winners, but the horse died before he could be delivered to the stable.[15] So devoted to racing was Goode that he had a racing path not only to the south of his manor house, but another, a mile course, to the north.[16] His brother Bennett Goode was to become a delegate and the object of satire in *The Patriots,* where he appears as Colonel Strut. Since John seems to have evidenced no political ambitions, the portrait here, if one exists, is a composite. But many prominent Mecklenburg gentlemen had their racehorses and presumably sent their mares to Baylor at Newmarket; the character is not detailed enough to suggest an original. For example, another prominent racing enthusiast, Henry Deloney, certainly qualifies for the particular quip: he sent a mare to Baylor to get "Old Harmless."[17] Although he did not have quite the string of horses which Goode owned, on 18 March he had "Godolphin" at stud.[18] He specialized in borrowing or otherwise acquiring the fastest horses and making bets against any horse the owner, or anyone else completely unaware of Deloney's nonce possession, could then produce. At least two such stories of Deloney have become racing classics, particularly that of "Polly Williams."[19] As "Colonel Simple" he was to become the object of satire in *The Patriots,* and as retiring sheriff at the time of the election, was already prominent in the political scene.

The coxcomb Strutabout is similarly a portrait with few particulars, but his original may have been a composite of the Speeds, who were certainly active politically. Joseph Speed was later to be satirized in *The Patriots;* but since he was born 27 March 1750, he would seem rather young to be campaigning for burgess in 1769 and 1770.[20] On the other hand he seems somewhat like Strutabout in his bellicose attitude. In March and April of 1771 both Thomas Evans and Humphry Hains instituted suit against him for assault and battery: whether these suits grew out of any electioneering fracas—or any fracas—does not appear.[21] But if the term "Jackanapes" suggests John among the Goodes, it might also suggest John Speed. The father, John Speed, Sr., ranked second only to Munford on the county commission; and in 1775 he was elected chairman of the Mecklenburg Committee, where his son John also served.[22] James, born in 1740, represented adjoining Charlotte County in the House of Burgesses from 1771 until the Revolution and was later elected delegate. He subsequently became one of the early judges in Kentucky, where according to family tradition, he "gave instructions in English branches and also Latin and Greek to his own and other children." "He had ready wit, wrote well, and was fond of writing humorous poetry. . . ."[23] Perhaps he also stood for Burgess in Mecklenburg County earlier and was the original of the coxcomb Strutabout. Strutabout's campaign manager, tavern keeper Jack Sly, may have been modelled upon John Speed, Jr., or upon Joseph or Lewis Speed, who were keeping the ordinary at their father's house about the time represented in the play.[24] Here again, then, although the unsuccessful candidates would have suggested originals to a local audience, Munford did not so particularize them that they could be recognized even at a Williamsburg performance. The satire was general rather than particular.

The freeholders are varied in their support of various candidates and in the warmth and disinterestedness of their support. Guzzle is dedicated equally to Sir John and to his vice of drink. Julip is hyperscrupulous: "My rule," he remarks to explain his absence from the barbecue, "is never to taste of a man's liquor unless I'm his friend, and therefore, I stay'd at home" (p. 44). Some are differentiated by their dialogue, as is Ned, a tool of Smallhopes, by his clipped speech.

One of the most striking features of *The Candidates* for one who is familiar with the traditional English satire of elections in fiction and drama is the position of the women. In addition to the farcical figure of Joan Guzzle, the wives of four freeholders have parts in the dialogue, and other country girls evidently appear in the play. One function the women serve is to provide the opportunity for some light, racy dialogue:

Lucy. Well, commend me to Mr. Wou'dbe, I say,—I nately like the man; he's mighty good to all his poor neighbours, and when he comes into a poor body's house, he's so free and so funny, isnt' he, old man? (*speaking to Twist*).
Twist. A little too free sometimes, faith; he was funny when he wanted to see the colour of your garters; wa'nt he?
Lucy. Oh! for shame, husband. Mr. Wou'dbe has no more harm about him, than a sucking babe; at least, if he has, I never saw it.
Twist. Nor felt it, I hope; . . . (pp. 25-26)

Soon afterwards Sir John, prompted by Guzzle, greets the freeholders by name:

Sir John. Hah! Mr. Roger Twist! your servant, sir. I hope your wife and children are well.
Twist. There's my wife. I have no children, at your service.
Sir John. A pretty girl: why, Roger, if you don't do better, you must call an old fellow to your assistance. (p. 28)

In the English political farces a mistress sometimes provides an extraneous romantic interest or a wife henpecks a husband into

political activity or inactivity, but there the dramatist was satirizing
a woman's interference in affairs outside her proper sphere. In *The
Candidates*, however, the women seem able to vote more intelli-
gently than can their husbands:

> *Lucy.* If the wives were to vote, I believe they would make a
> better choice than their husbands.
> *Twist.* You'd be for the funnyest—wou'dn't you?
> *Lucy.* Yes, faith; and the wittiest, and prettiest, and the wisest, and
> the best too; you are all for ugly except when you chose me.
> *Catherine.* Well done, Lucy, you are right, girl. If we were all to
> speak to our old men as freely as you do, there would be better doings.
> (p. 26)

The least important character in the play is Wou'dbe's servant
Ralpho. Some freak of common misunderstanding has made him
seem the most important character, historically, in the play. Hailed
by historians of the theater as America's first stage Negro, he
was never intended for a Negro at all. In the cast of characters he
is bracketed with an innkeeper and another freeholder. He does
not appear on stage with the Negroes in the scene in which breakfast is served at Wou'dbe's home. He refers to himself as a "poor
servant" and to his "faithful service" in the language of an indentured servant rather than that of a slave; and he refers to John
Guzzle only as "neighbor Guzzle" (p. 21). When he begs a cast-
off suit from Wou'dbe, he wishes to "make a figure among the
girls this Election" (p. 16). The girls, who are included in the
cast of characters, would not be Negro slaves, but daughters of
the freeholders. Ralpho, moreover, does not speak in the slightest
in Negro dialect, though in his "Letters from the Devil" Munford
showed clearly that he could differentiate Negro speech (p. 194).
His use of malapropisms did not anticipate pretentious Negro
speech; it followed the practice of innumerable characters in Shakespeare, eighteenth century fiction, Termagant in Arthur Murphy's
Upholsterer (1758), and perhaps Mrs. Malaprop herself in *The
Rivals*: "Gadse! this figure of mine is not reconsiderable in its
delurements, and when I'm dressed out like a gentleman, the girls,
I'm a thinking, will find me desistible" (p. 16).

Probably the mistake in coloring Ralpho arose from the delusion
that in Colonial and Revolutionary Virginia house servants were
all Negroes. Even if they all had been, Munford did not always
perfectly adapt the traditions of English comedy to the Virginia scene. For example, when in the opening scene Ralpho an-
nounces that Sir John is "below," Munford is visualizing traditional
English stage practice. In Virginia, drawing room and library

were on the main, or ground floor. But as a glance at the Virginia *Gazette* will show, the system of employing indentured white servants in Munford's day was still widespread in Virginia. They not only taught school and worked in skilled trades but they also acted as common domestics. If *The Candidates* did not in itself offer adequate indication of Ralpho's white color, such confirmation is unmistakable in *The Patriots*. There the list of white domestics is quite extensive: Pickle, servant to Meanwell and one of the two principal heroes, actually a nephew incognito; Meanwell's butler, who poses as an Anglican clergyman; the cook; the scullion; the groom; and another servant: all are intended witnesses to the sham marriage with which Pickle is attempting to seduce Melinda. Since the servants are obviously white in *The Patriots*, why should Ralpho be blackfaced? Munford does not need to rely for fame upon such a mistaken priority.

In dramatizing an election Munford was utilizing material of perennial fascination for eighteenth century novelists and dramatists. English fiction particularly is full of this material. The most complete satire on corrupt election practices is *Flagel: or a Ramble of Fancy through the Land of Electioneering* (1768). Here is to be found varied satire on elections contested and uncontested. Fake news items satirize overeating and drinking during the hustings and announce several members of Parliament "as good as new" "*To be Sold to the Best Bidder*." A company of woolcombers advertises for candidates for the Borough of ——— ———, stating the necessary promises, obviously a satire upon the notorius offer made that year by members of the Oxford City Council. In one scene the incumbent of an uncontested seat writes the mayor, the aldermen, and their wives and daughters of his favor and sends them a whole buck; he appears only at the time of a general election to give a dinner and get the whole corporation drunk. Finally one agent is seen slipping five guineas into a tradesman's pocket, and another is mentioned who "can transfer a competent number of names from one side of the book to the other, so as to secure a clear majority in favour of which side he pleases."[25] Electioneering scenes are vivid and detailed also in Smollett's *Peregrine Pickle* (1751) and *Sir Launcelot Greaves* (1760-62) and in Charles Johnston's *Chrysal* (1760-1765) and *The Reverie* (1763).

But among the most vivid and humorous scenes of electioneering in eighteenth century satire are those in Fielding's dramas *Don Quixote in England* (1734) and *Pasquin* (1736). Inimitable is the honest mayor's attempt, in the former, to dig up even a crazy opponent for Sir Thomas Loveland so that "when both parties have spent as much as they are able, every honest man will vote according to his conscience."[26] In the latter, especially in "The Election," so biting is the criticism of open bribery that the scene hastened the censorship of the stage and drove political satire into fiction. In drama, political satire after censorship perforce became relatively innocuous. *The Election, a Comedy of Three Acts* (1749), a fairly amusing anonymous farce, avoided realistic characterization and offense to authority by being written as a puppet drama. Miles Peter Andrews' brief *New Musical Interlude called the Election* (1774) is not a satire and contains nothing of consequence which could have attracted Munford except perhaps the patriotic father's anticipation of Patrick Henry: "Each free-born Briton's song should be,/'Or give me Death or Liberty!' "[27] Henry Bate Dudley's *Rival Candidates* (1775) exhibits some similarities to *The Patriots*, but provides no sharp election satire and provided no material for *The Candidates*. After Fielding, only Foote's *Mayor of Garratt* (1764) seems sharp and pointed enough to have provided any material for Munford's electioneering play. Although Douglass' American Company was presenting Foote's play at least as early as 1771, the setting and characters are quite different.

Much of this satire in English fiction and drama Munford was surely familiar with. But he seems deliberately to have avoided presenting a familiar type of sensational election—a protested one. Perhaps it would have hit too near home. Munford must have known of the public disgrace meted out to his own father. In 1736 his uncle Richard Bland complained that Robert Munford the dramatist's father had been unduly returned as burgess; and on 1 September 1736 the father had to stand at his place in the House of Burgesses and receive a public reprimand for interfering with the inquiry into this complaint.[28] The dramatist's first committee appointment as a burgess was to chair a committee ordered to investigate the charge of Henry Delony that the election of Edmund Taylor, Munford's first colleague from Mecklenburg County, was undue.[29] Several relatives had more recently been involved in protested elections. On 7 November 1766 Munford's brother-in-law William Fitzhugh, of Stafford, complained of the undue election of Thompson Mason, then withdrew the plea.[30] On 12 May 1769 Munford's first cousin Theoderick Bland petitioned the House against the undue election and return of Peter Poythress.[31] Moreover, in the very year in which the play is set, 1770, Munford was acting in Halifax County as chairman of a subcommittee examining into the election and return of Nathaniel Terry. He submitted a report which severely censured the conduct of Terry;[32] and Munford evidently wanted to avoid the consequences of using material which might too obviously suggest this sensational election or might recall the protested elections in which his own relatives had been involved.

If, however, Munford's *Candidates* was less sensational than it could have been, it was more universal and more meaningful. One aspect of elections which the author did not avoid or exaggerate was the consumption of alcohol which evidently accompanied any election, English or Colonial, contested or uncontested. Guzzle, it will be recalled, appears drinking heavily at the opening of the play and gradually gets drunker. His wife, John, and Sir John lose consciousness. Even at Mr. Wou'dbe's modest breakfast, intoxicants make their appearance on hustings day. "Boy, give me the spirit," Mr. Julip orders. "This chocolate, me thinks, wants a little lacing to make it admirable" (p. 47). Many perceptive Virginians deplored the practice of "swilling the planters with bumbo," as cousin Theoderick Bland put it.[33] But even George Washington was not above complying with the practice, as can be seen from the list of liquor consumed at his expense during his election campaign in Winchester while he and Munford were on the expedition against Fort Duquesne: 28 gallons of rum, 40 gallons and 10 bowls of rum punch, 34 gallons of wine, 46 gallons of beer, and other potent potables.[34]

In Southside Virginia the custom of swilling the freeholders was well established before Munford arrived. In 1757 Matthew Marrable attempted to set aside the election of Thomas Nash in Lunenburg County on the charge of treats and entertainments after the writ for the election. But the official report made 7 May 1757 found that "before the Poll began, a Tickler of Rum was by the Ordinary-Keeper, by Order of Mr *Marrable*, delivered to one Man, and a Bottle of Rum to some others, who were preparing a Barbeque. That the Liquor delivered at the Ordinary, during the Poll, was charged to the Candidate in whose Name it was demanded; and Mr *Marrable's* and Mr *Embry's* Accounts were the largest."[35] Evidently Marrable's "agents" were especially active in standing drinks. The following year, on 16 September 1758, Marrable's election was contested by Henry Blagrave. The report caused Marrable to be unseated: ". . . the Morning of the Election Liquor was distributed to the Company of Mr *Marrable*, by his Orders, but with this Caution, To take Care they should not intoxicate themselves, least a Riot might ensue at the Election, because he wanted a fair Poll, and every Candidate to stand or fall by his own interest; and Mr *Marrable* declared he expended seven Weathers, and thirty Gallons of Rum on that occasion. . . ."[36] The moral is put a bit sententiously by Worthy: "I'm sorry, my countrymen, for the sake of a little toddy, can be induced to behave in a manner so contradictory to the candour and integrity which always should prevail among mankind" (p. 45).

Fisticuffs, another frequent accompaniment of the political campaign, add excitement to the play. In England the candidate himself was ordinarily above this sort of thing. Use of the fists stamped a man as a blackguard, though with the appearance of Broughton the art of boxing became acceptable socially perhaps as a means of self-protection. Munford's hero, Wou'dbe, a gentleman, eschews the use of his fists when, bettered in argument, Strutabout offers a resort to force:

> *Strutabout.* I can lick you, Wou'be. (*beginning to strip.*)
> *Wou'dbe.* You need not strip to do it; for you intend to do it with your tongue, I suppose.
> *Smallhopes.* (*clapping Strutabout upon the back*) Well done Strutabout,—you can do it, by God. Don't be afraid, you shan't be hurt; damn me if you shall, (*strips.*)
>
> . . . .
>
> *1st Freeholder.* Up to him—I'll stand by you. (*to Wou'dbe.*)
> *2d Freeholder.* They are not worth your notice, Mr. Wou'dbe; but if you have a mind to try yourself, I'll see fair play.
> *Wou'dbe.* When I think they have sufficiently exposed themselves, I'll explain the opinion I have of them, with the end of my cain. (pp. 35, 36)

Here Munford may have been remembering some of the details of the sensational Terry-Coles campaign in 1769 in Halifax County. In the report of this election, submitted originally by Munford's subcommittee, the Sheriff explained why he was unable to conduct a poll:

> . . . I said, I would read the Writ; And having it in my Hands for that Purpose, Mr Terry came to me, his Coat and his Waistcoat being stripped off, and his Collar Open, and holding up a large Stick, threatened to cane me, and declared, if I attempted to read the Writ, he would split me down, and did aim, and endeavour several Times to strike me, as I was about to read the Writ (according to what I thought my Duty) with his Stick, which, the Blows being warded off by People between us, did not touch my Person, that I remember, but fell upon the Writ in my Hands. Immediately after this such a Tumult ensued, and the Electors were in such a Temper, and so disorderly, and some of them drank of spiritous Liquors to such Excess,

*that I was convinced a fair Election could not have been made after-
wards on that Day: . . .*[37]

To make the fisticuffs more farcical, Munford burlesqued the
motif in the final scene, with Guzzle:

> *1st Freeholder.* Sir, I won't be called a fool by any man, I'll have
> you to know, sir.
> *Guzzle.* Then you oughn't to be one; but here's at ye, adrat ye,
> if ye're for a quarrel. Sir John Toddy would have stood a good chance,
> and I'll maintain it, come on, damn ye.
> *1st Freeholder.* Oh! as for fighting, there I'm your servant; a drunk-
> ard is as bad to fight as a madman. (*runs off.*)
> *Guzzle.* Houroa, houroa, you see no body so good at a battle as a
> staunch toper, The milksops are afraid of them to a man.
> *3d Freeholder.* You knew he was a coward before you thought
> proper to attack him; if you think yourself so brave, try your hand
> upon me, and you'll find you're mistaken.
> *Guzzle.* For the matter of that, I'm the best judge myself; good
> day, my dear, good day. Huzza, for Sir John Toddy. [*Exit.*] (p. 49)

Here again Munford may have been recalling the Halifax election,
where one of the candidates played the role of the third Freeholder:
". . . after this interruption, Mr *Coles* came up and told the said
Hopkins, if he was hindered in the Execution of his Office he
knew what kind of Return to make, and if the said *Terry* wanted
to cane any Person, let him cane him; which Words the said *Lyne*
believes the said *Terry* did not hear, as he did not then take any
Notice of them. . . ."[38]

But Munford did not have to go to the next county for physical
violence at an election. A report of the committee examining the
1758 Marrable-Blagrave election in Lunenburg censured the conduct of John Hobson, "which was very illegal and tumultous, in
offering to lay Wagers the Poll was closed when it was not; in
proclaiming at the Court-house Door the Poll was going to be
closed, and desiring the Freeholders to come in and vote, and
then violently, by striking and kicking at them, preventing them
from so doing, by which Means many Freeholders did not vote
at the said Election."[39]

All these farcical materials add zest to what otherwise might
have been too serious for a dramatic afterpiece. But the proposal
and the election of the proper candidates are, after all, the central
material of the play. The duty of the properly qualified man
to offer himself is sounded by Wou'dbe in the opening lines: "Must
I again be subject to the humours of a fickle croud? Must I again

resign my reason, and be nought but what each voter pleases? Must I cajole, fawn, and wheedle, for a place that brings so little profit?" (p. 13). When Worthy finally agrees to stand a poll, the theme is the same:

> *Worthy.* I have little inclination to the service; you know my aversion to a public life, Wou'dbe, and how little I have ever courted the people for the troublesome office they have hitherto imposed upon me.
>
> *Wou'dbe.* I believe you enjoy as much domestic happiness as any person, and that your aversion to a public life proceeds from the pleasure you find at home. But, sir, it surely is the duty of every man who has abilities to serve his country, to take up the burden, and bear it with patience. (p. 42)

Wou'dbe is concerned at Worthy's reluctance to campaign. Although he asks Worthy only to show himself to the people, he soliloquizes: "It would give me great pleasure if Worthy would be more anxious than he appears to be upon this occasion; conscious of his abilities and worth, he scorns to ask a vote for any person but me . . ." (p. 43). This duty of accepting and even seeking public office is enforced by the action of the play as well as by the words of the sententious Wou'dbe: before Worthy enters the campaign, Wou'dbe is in difficulties; afterwards, when two able candidates support each other, the outcome is certain.

The other central theme is the selection of the proper candidate. Here Munford uses ably the motifs, first, of malicious rumors deliberately spread by the opposition; and more important, of the campaign promise. Full enjoyment of the irony involved necessitates our knowledge of Munford's own legislative achievements. For example, some of the freeholders question Wou'dbe concerning the new taxes:

> *Guzzle.* Suppose, Mr. Wou'dbe, we were to want you to get the price of rum lower'd—wou'd you do it?
>
> *Wou'dbe.* I cou'd not.
>
> *Guzzle.* Huzza for Sir John! he has promised to do it, huzza for Sir John!
>
> *Twist.* Suppose, Mr. Wou'dbe, we should want this tax taken off— cou'd you do it?
>
> *Wou'dbe.* I could not.
>
> *Twist.* Huzza for Mr. Strutabout! he's damn'd, if he don't. Huzza for Mr. Strutabout! (p. 31)

Wou'dbe is risking votes in failing to promise to attack a necessary tax, one which Munford doubtless approved—a tax of a penny per gallon placed on rum imported from April, 1769 until April, 1783, a tax rendered necessary by the state of the treasury after the disclosure of Speaker Robinson's misappropriations. Munford may have remembered also the voters in Foote's *Mayor of Garratt*. There Matthew Mug is discredited as a candidate "because, d'ye see, state affairs would not jog glibly without laying a farthing a quart upon ale; this scoundrel, not contented to take things in a medium way, has had the impudence to raise it a penny."[40]

Concerning the next campaign promise, ferriage, Munford was providing a laugh at his own expense:

Stern. Suppose, Mr. Wou'dbe, we that live over the river, should want to come to church on this side, is it not very hard we should pay ferryage; when we pay as much to the church as you do?
Wou'dbe. Very hard.
Stern. Suppose we were to petition the assembly could you get us clear of that expence?
Wou'dbe. I believe it to be just; and make no doubt but it would pass into a law.
Stern. Will you do it?
Wou'dbe. I will endeavour to do it. (p. 31)

The irony of the situation is that on 4 December 1767 Munford did introduce into the House a bill to exempt the inhabitants of Mecklenburg County from the payment of ferriage on Sundays, court days, and days of general muster. On 11 April 1767 it passed into law.[41] The jest is that on 18 November 1769 another petition from Mecklenburg County asked for the repeal of the same law! Presented originally when Munford was absent, a bill repealing Munford's was presented by Bland and Matthew Marrable, and it was finally passed while Munford was absent.[42]

On another campaign issue the hero refuses to commit himself:

Prize. Why don't you burgesses, do something with the damn'd pickers? If we have a hogshead of tobacco refused, away it goes to them; and after they have twisted up the best of it for their own use, and taken as much as will pay for their trouble, the poor planter has little for his share.
Wou'dbe. There are great complaints against them; and I believe the assembly will take them under consideration.
Prize. Will you vote against them?
Wou'dbe. I will, if they deserve it.
Prize. Huzza for Mr. Wou'dbe! (pp. 31-32)

Here Munford had Wou'dbe refuse to make a definite commitment perhaps because he felt that the pickers were, after all, necessary.

An early petition of 13 March 1761 had protested against them, citing "the illegal and oppressive Behavior" and "praying that these Evils may be prevented by an Act to restrain the Pickers to a certain limited Number, to be nominated by the County-Courts."[43] Thus the issue was no new one. Munford was probably recalling, however, a later petition, of 19 March 1767, from Louisa County for an act to "suspend the present Pickers of Tobacco, and to prohibit any others for the future."[44] The petition was tabled and died.

At the end of the play the sheriff declares Worthy and Wou'dbe elected, and they are brought on stage in a manner traditional for election comedies—raised aloft, on chairs, upon the shoulders of the freeholders. Captain Paunch is given the final lines:

> . . . we have done as we ought, we have elected the ablest, according to the writ.
>> Henceforth, let those who pray for wholesome laws,
>> And all well-wishers to their country's cause,
>> Like us refuse a coxcomb—choose a man—
>> Then let our senate blunder if it can. (pp. 50-51)

The action and the words of the play thus end with a tone of optimism, a faith in the democratic process far different from that disillusioned tone apparent in Brackenridge's *Modern Chivalry*. The moral obligation of *noblesses oblige* is here dramatically presented, an ideal which the Virginia gentleman brought with him from England and which helped to vitalize Virginia and Southern politics until *noblesse oblige* degenerated into special privilege rather than increased responsibility and until the Southern aristocrat left the field of politics to the red-necked lawyer.

VI

Dramatist: *The Patriots*

THE PATRIOTS deserves attention not merely because it is America's first legitimate comedy, but because in it Munford dramatizes with originality and artistry a problem which is particularly American.

Like *The Candidates*, *The Patriots* was evidently first printed by his son, William, in 1798. The "1776 Philadelphia" edition referred to by Quinn and others is a ghost edition.[1] No record of any performance has been noted; the play was probably never produced. The First Continental Congress had in 1774 discouraged the presentation of plays;[2] and Munford here took great liberties with fairly well-known personalities of Southside Virginia and presented a moderate view which his neighbors would doubtless have found unpatriotic. But possibly he aimed at and arranged for a private performance, though surely not at Sir Peyton Skipwith's Prestwould, which probably housed the "theatre" in Mecklenburg County where William Munford later enacted the role of Archer, in Farquhar's *Recruiting Officer*—the favorite comedy of Colonial America.[3]

The earliest possible date of composition is the time of the setting—1777. At the opening of the play, news of the victory at Trenton, on Christmas Day, 1776, has just been announced, presumably in the Virginia *Gazette*, and later in the play there arrives news of the subsequent victory at Princeton. The play seems to glance at the trial of the Scottish merchants in the Mecklenburg Court in April, 1777; the subsequent petition of 14 May 1777, sent the House of Delegates by the freeholders of Mecklenburg to protest against the lenient handling of the Scots; and the Virginia loyalty oath of May, 1777. Nothing in the play suggests that Munford could not have begun and even finished it in that year, but it was probably completed somewhat later. The good humor, serenity, and optimism may suggest that he completed it in 1779, after he was re-elected to the House of Delegates. It was probably written before 1780. Our hero Meanwell suggests to Mr. Summons,

"Be a colonel of militia then, 'tis a fine post for cripples, for they never march . . ." (p. 70). The laugh would not have been in good taste after the rout of the Virginia militia at Camden on 14 August 1780. Nor was Munford in a lighthearted mood after that date. Nor did he again have the leisure he enjoyed before Camden—until he was embittered, ill, and dying.

In *The Patriots*, utilizing a traditionally complex plot for his vehicle, Munford created characters who incorporate at once local caricatures and traditional, general types to dramatize a theme of universal significance—the nature of loyalty.

The plot is of a kind popular in eighteenth century English comedy. It embodies three romances, the first farcical, the second comic, and the third serious. The farcical plot is the abortive romance of Colonel Strut and Isabella, "a female politician." A militant patriot, Isabella is "resolved not to love a man who knows nothing of war and Washington" (p. 60). ". . . I am in love with nothing but my country," she asserts. "If, indeed, a man should approach me, who would lay his laurels at my feet, who could count his glorious scars gained in the front of victory, I might look upon him" (p. 61). To prosecute his suit, Colonel Strut has got himself elected delegate to the Convention and has been made a colonel of militia. But the suit comes to a farcical conclusion when Isabella propels the Colonel into a quarrel with Flash, a recruiting officer and, like Strut, a coward:

Strut. What! quarrel with a madman? The man is deranged in his mind. Are you not frantic, sir?

Flash. Frantic, my name Frantic! D—mn you, sir, I'll not be nick-named by any scoundrel living.

Isa. Scoundrel! now we shall have it, draw, colonel. (*She takes Strut's hand, and puts it upon the hilt of his sword.*)

Strut. He did not call me scoundrel, madam. He only said he would not be nick-named by any scoundrel living. I have not nick-named him, madam.

Flash. It is a lie, sir.

Isa. What say you to that, colonel?

Strut. The man is mad, absolutely mad, madam.

Flash. Blood and fire.

Isa. (*Draws Struts sword and puts it in his hand.*) Now, colonel.

Flash. A pretty blade, let's see it my dear.

Isa. Let him feel it, colonel. Up to him. (*pushes up Strut.*)

Flash. (*puts up his own sword, and advances to look at that of Strut.*) With your leave, my dear, from France, no doubt. I have heard they are all the best polishers in the world.

Strut. Stand off, sir; what did you mean by calling me a scoundrel?

Flash. I call you a scoundel! Upon my soul, my dear, you are
disordered in your mind.

. . . . . .

Strut. You hear, madam; he did not give me the lie.

Isab. Was there ever such a paltry coward! to put up with such
an affront, and then stand parleying with a fellow who only apologizes
for it, by abusing his mistress? give me the sword. (*Takes the sword
and runs at Flash.*)

Flash. A man in petticoats, by God! oh, ho! my dear, I smell a
rat. Yes, yes, honey, catch Flash if you can. Two to one! Oh! no, no,
my dear; I'll not be assassinated by God. (*runs off.*) (pp. 110-112)

The original of Colonel Strut was probably Colonel Bennett
Goode, who had been born in Goochland County in 1745-1746
and had moved to Mecklenburg County as a young man.[4] Although before 1775 he had never been named on the county commission, he was in that year named second on the Mecklenburg
Committee of Observation,[5] and during 1775 and 1776 he was
regularly elected to the Virginia Convention, evidently defeating
Munford in 1775 in a bitterly contested election. Somehow he had
obtained his colonelcy.[6] He was evidently the first signer and
perhaps the originator of a petition against the Scottish merchants.[7]
Interestingly enough Bennett Goode actually did marry an Isabella,
the daughter of Howell Lewis, of Granville County, North Carolina.[8] Lewis was a man of some station; he represented Granville
County in the legislature, was a dashing cavalry officer, and, by
the end of the war, was the lieutenant colonel in command of the
Hillsborough Cavalry Regiment.[9] Knowing these circumstances, a
Southside audience would have relished Colonel Strut's response
when Isabella stipulates that her accepted suitor must attain the
rank of general. "I can apply in a neighboring state," the Colonel
timidly suggests, obviously indicating Isabella's North Carolina,
"and be made a brigadier-general, without being a soldier" (p. 87).

Munford has deliberately altered and heightened the picture,
and his Isabella may resemble the real Mrs. Goode only in her
patriotism. Goode and Isabella Howell, moreover, were married
about 1770-years before the period in which the play is set.[10] But
Munford evidently created Isabella from hints in Mrs. Goode, from
Melinda in *The Recruiting Officer*, Biddy in Garrick's *Miss in Her
Teens*, and most of all from the exigencies of the role she was to
play in the plot and the development of the theme.

Obviously the mock duel goes back far into English and even
Roman dramatic tradition, where the figure of the braggart soldier
had already become established as a comic type. One of the best

known, Captain Bobadill, appears in Jonson's *Every Man in his Humour*, a play which was performed in Williamsburg on 23 November 1771 as the first recorded performance of a Jonson play in Colonial America.[11] Munford may have attended the performance; at least he was absent from meetings of the Mecklenburg Court during November and December. Or perhaps a nearer precedent, in view of Flash's remark about a man in petticoats, may have been *Twelfth Night*, which furnishes a similar pair of reluctant duellists, one of them Viola, dressed as a man. Brazen, in Farquhar's *Recruiting Officer*, was not a pattern here: Brazen is no coward. But Flash in Garrick's *Miss in Her Teens*, a farce popular with Virginia audiences, probably was. There too the heroine vainly attempts to arrange a duel between Flash, "a fine blust'ring Man" who is "always talking of Fighting, and Wars,"[12] and another suitor, Fribble. Garrick's farce may also have suggested the name of Squib, another Munford character.[13] There are additional parallels between the two plays. Munford's Flash courts Mira with his sword, drawing, lunging, and flourishing it:

Flash. Noble, by God! d—m me! here's the stuff, (*drawing his sword*) shall make the cowardly dogs skip, we'll let the scoundrels see what Americans can do. . . .

. . . . .

Mars, I adore thee; Mars, was a fellow of spirit, I'm told, the Flash of his day, I warrant it. By God, I wish the lad was here now, that he and I might have a game at tilts together: (*draws his sword and pushes at the wall.*) Ha, ha; there I had him! I'god, now I cou'd gizzard these English dogs, if I had 'em here. (pp. 63-64).

So also does Garrick's Flash court Miss Biddy:

Flash. I never do, Madam; it is not my Method of Proceeding; here's my Logic? [*Draws his sword.*] Sa, sa—my best Argument is Cart over Arm, Madam, ha, ha; [*lunges,*] and if he answers that, Madam, through my small Guts, my Breath, Blood and Mistress are all at his Service— —

. . . . .

. . . Lookee, Miss, I'm a Man of Honour; Glory's my Aim, I have told you the Road I am in, and do you see here, Child, [*Shewing his Sword.*] no Tricks upon Travellers.[14]

This subplot is rather loosely tied in with the other plots. Isabella is an acquaintance of the principal heroine, Mira; and Colonel Strut is a member of the committee which examines the hero on a charge of disloyalty. But even here, in the least important plot of all, are ridiculed the extremes of rabid patriotism in Isabella and cowardice in Colonel Strut. The first subplot admirably and amusingly dramatizes one aspect of Munford's thesis of loyalty.

The second subplot offers disguise, brisk dialogue, and farce. Here Pickle, Meanwell's genteel white servant, poses as the master himself and attempts to seduce Melinda Heartfree, an attractive country girl. Peregrine Pickle, one recalls, in Smollett's novel attempts to seduce his Emilia; and from her letters Elizabeth Munford at least, shows a familiarity with this novel. But here the affair is conducted in a lighter vein. Some of the comic possibilities implicit in the seduction Munford employs quite capably. For example Pickle attempts to explain why he wishes to fondle her:

Pick. I only wish to examine my commodity before I purchase. (*taking her hand*) I wish to know more of you, my dear.

. . . . . .

. . . The liberties I wish to take, my dear, are licensed freedoms. Love requires something of this kind to keep itself alive. 'Tis as necessary to love as fuel is to fire. If you don't let me toy and play with you a little, by my soul, my love will go out. (p. 89.)

Possibly Munford got his idea here from Farquhar's *Recruiting Officer*, where Plume explains why he is trying to obtain Sylvia for a mistress instead of a wife:

. . . I'm resolv'd never to bind my self to a Woman for my whole Life, till I know whether I shall like her Company for half an Hour— Suppose I marry'd a Woman that wanted a Leg? Such a thing might be, unless I examin'd the Goods before-hand; if People wou'd but try one another's Constitutions before they engag'd, it wou'd prevent all those Elopements, Divorces, and the Devil knows what.[15]

Perhaps Munford remembered also Cibber's *Damon and Phillida*, a one act opera popular at Williamsburg. He may have owed something to the scene in which Damon courts Phillida for a mistress rather than a wife: "What! not a Hand, a Lip, for old Acquaintance? Not one poor Sample of the Grain, my Dear, Unless I make a Purchase of the whole?"[16]

In order to seduce Melinda, Pickle arranges a sham marriage, to be performed by Meanwell's reluctant butler and witnessed by the other servants:

Butler. What am I to do?
Pick. Be all gravity, sir, and with a demure face and most audible voice, read the ceremony.
Butler. The ceremony! where must I find it?
Pick. Here, sir, (*opens the book*) you are to begin here.

But. Yes, yes, how much is there of it?
Pick. All this. (*shews him*)
But. Why it would take me a month to read all that—
Pick. Zounds! man, can't you read?
But. Great D-e-a-r, dear, l-y-ly, darly, b-e, be, l-o, lo, belo, v-e-d, ved, beloved, darly beloved.
Pick. Pish! try here.
But. Great W-i-l-t,- wilt, t-h-o-u, tho' h-a—
Pick. Hush you clodheaded fool; here comes Melinda. (p. 118)

As Pickle explains to her, his clergyman has an impediment in his speech.

For his slow reader who spells out successively the letter, the syllable, and the word, Munford may have developed the hint of Sir Timorous, in Dryden's *Wild Gallant;* a nearer pattern, however, would have been the Yorkshire squire Sapscull, in Henry Carey's *Honest Yorkshire-Man* (1736), a ballad farce popular at Williamsburg. In this play Sapscull makes out an address with considerable difficulty: "Letter says, G-r-o-z-Groz-v-e-ve-n-e-r-neer Grozveneer Square. . . ."[17] Whatever his source, Munford certainly made amusing use of the device. He shows considerable artistry in making ludicrous the fake marriage, which at first threatens to become so serious as to ruin the comic tone. Here the tone is so lightened that it resembles the mood in Charles Coffey's *Female Parson, or Beau in the Suds* (1730), or in *As You Like It,* where the audience is not really alarmed for Audrey's virtue, despite the fact that Touchstone is providing a questionable priest, Sir Oliver Martext: "I am not in the mind but I were better to be married of him than of another; for he is not like to marry me well; and not being well married, it will be a good excuse for me hereafter to leave my wife" (III, iii, 78-81).

When his attempt to dupe Melinda is thwarted through betrayal by the servants and the arrival of Meanwell, Pickle is willing to marry her; here, moreover, Pickle strips off his incognito and reveals himself as the wealthy and aristocratic young Worthy. The subplot thus seems to take on a truly democratic, American tone, where love ignores rank and rewards virtue. But so to interpret this reversal of Pickle would be to misunderstand him; his proper evaluation of true love even in seemingly humble form comes more from sentimental English comedy than from American practice. In his *Conscious Lovers* (1722) Steele provided only one of the best known examples of the ability of the hero to recognize and reward virtue, and there, as here, his unselfish constancy paid dividends. As Joseph Wood Krutch re-

marked in his *Comedy and Conscience After the Restoration.*
"Nothing is more characteristic of sentimental comedy than this
sudden discovery that a disinterested sacrifice made nobly turns
out to be no sacrifice at all."[18] For in a sentimental recognition scene
the penniless country lass Melinda is revealed by the Heartfrees as
Miss Spendall, Meanwell's niece, left with poor country people by
her dying mother so that the girl would avoid the vices of her spend-
thrift father and receive the virtuous education of rural innocence.
This idea of rusticated aristocratic virtue also, just as English as
it is American, can be found for example in Charles Johnson's
Country Lasses (1753), where the father, who has squandered his
estate, retires to the country so that there he can bring up his
daughters properly and they will be sought for their virtue rather
than for their dowry.

For his romantic comedian George ("Pickle") Worthy, Esq.,
of Maryland, Munford may have had in mind the attractive young
rakes of fiction like Peregrine Pickle and of Restoration drama like
Farquhar's Plume and especially his Archer. The inconsistency
in the characterization—from the Restoration rake in the opening
scenes to the sentimental wooer in the final scene—would hardly
bother any audience accustomed to sentimental comedy. Melinda
too comes from English dramatic tradition of the eighteenth century rather than from Southside Virginia; she has perhaps a touch
of Cherry in Farquhar's *Beaux Strategem*, and her name probably
comes from *The Recruiting Officer.*

Of the three romances in *The Patriots*, the principal or straight
one, that of Trueman and Mira, is the most conventional, the least
colorful. This lack of color frequently characterizes the principal
romance in an eighteenth century comedy. Here, however, the
romance is given additional importance by being closely inter-
twined with the thematic, political action—the examination of the
principal hero on the charge of toryism. In the opening lines of
the play this mutual interdependence of plot and theme is announced:

Mean. What? are you too accused of toryism?
True. I am indeed. . . . And what is worse, I fear the consequences
will be serious, and a little uncommon.
Mean. How?
True. They will be bad indeed if they cause the loss of the girl
I love. (p. 55)

Earlier Mira has been betrothed to Trueman; but Brazen, Mira's
father, a violent whig and a member of the local Committee of

Observation, is determined that no tory will ever marry his daughter. Indeed he suggests that his daughter marry Captain Flash, an active patriot, a recruiting officer. Mira retains her faith in her lover, and with the help of the intermediary Pickle they plan to elope. This romantic recourse proves unnecessary. Captain Flash shows himself to be a coward; Tackabout, who has accused Trueman and Meanwell of toryism, proves to be himself the tory; and Trueman is reinstated as a loyal American and the proper suitor for Mira. The play thus ends with a double wedding.

In the play Mira not only performs the role of principal heroine, but serves a thematic function as well. Like the hero, she embodies a golden mean between cowardice and the rabid militancy exemplified by Isabella. She is thus contrasted with Isabella, the female patriot. Mira believes that "the smiles of beauty should reward the man who bravely asserts his country's rights, and meets her enemies in the bloody field" (p. 60). But she does not relish gore and scars for their own sakes. Neither Trueman nor Mira seems to suggest a Virginia counterpart; her name Munford may have adopted from Lord Lansdowne's "Mira."

Among the subsidiary roles in this plot, the characterization of Brazen, Mira's father, is similar to that of a typical stage squire, or perhaps to Squire Western of *Tom Jones*. According to Trueman, "Her father is a violent patriot without knowing the meaning of the word. He understands little or nothing beyond a dice-box and race-field, but thinks he knows every thing; and woe be to him that contradicts him! His political notions are a system of perfect anarchy, but he reigns in his own family with perfect despotism" (p. 56). Munford probably did not intend in Brazen to satirize a particular Virginia neighbor. Much of his character seems necessitated by the dual role he must play as a member of the Committee and as heavy father, in which latter role he resembles Ballance in Farquhar's *Recruiting Officer*, though there the father's opposition to the hero is financial rather than political.

Another minor character, Flash, as has been seen, is utilized in the Isabella-Colonel Strut subplot to prove the Colonel a coward and in the principal plot to prepare Trueman's restoration to favor by demonstrating Flash's own cowardice. This double function perhaps justifies the inclusion of comic recruiting scenes by his sergeant, Trim. They are so amusing that one would not wish them away, and recruiting was pertinent satirical material for a play dramatizing the theme of loyalty. Trim explains to Flash his failure to secure recruits:

Why, sir, I got ten clever fellows to promise me to enlist (*hickups*) do you see me, just as the brandy gave out, they kept punctually calling for more grog, I told them, says I, (*hickups*) I am very sorry, says I, the brandy is out. e'god, sir, the words were no sooner out of my mouth, (*hickups*) than away they went, every soul of them. (p. 81)

Though the parallels are by no means close, Munford was probably inspired to the use of this material by the brilliantly successful recruiting scenes of Plume and Kite in Farquhar's *Recruiting Officer*. Trim doubtless got his name from Richard Steele's comedy *The Funeral*, which was in Douglass' repertoire, rather than from *Tristram Shandy*.

It is unlikely that Mecklenburg County furnished originals for Flash and Trim, though various men were active in recruiting there: William and Thomas Lewis, Samuel Hopkins, Austen Petillo, and William Goddin.[19] One of the most interesting incidents in Mecklenburg recruiting came after the General Assembly of May 1780 arranged for the appointment of recruiting officers in the various districts of each county. Austen Petillo, one of the officers for Mecklenburg County, agreed with William Goddin to pay him £10,000 for recruiting, to be collected from the exempts. As County Lieutenant, Munford, however, rightly refused to sanction any such authority for Goddin. Obviously Goddin and Petillo came too late to inspire the roles of Trim and Flash. Perhaps others earlier had recruited in Mecklenburg County in the time-honored fashion employed by Falstaff and Farquhar's Plume, preying upon those who obviously would buy off—would pay for a substitute. The recruiting officer would then pocket the money and send to the field of battle a motley crew like Falstaff's. Or perhaps Munford kept such officers out of the county. But this scandal of recruiting certainly pervaded the rest of Virginia. According to Eckenrode, "an army of commissaries and recruiting officers supported themselves on the State by sheer plunder."[20]

The inclusion of Flash and Trim is intended also to ridicule the role played in recruiting by the local Committee for Observation. Recruiting immediately became an area of intense activity throughout Virginia, and it was the subject of the very first resolution passed by the Mecklenburg Committee: "*Resolved unanimously, that every member of this committee exert his endeavours to enlist volunteer soldiers, agreeable to the resolution of the late Provincial Convention.*"[21] Such an activity continued to be a major objective of the local Committees.[22] In December of 1775 the local Committees were given the responsibility of nominating a captain and another officer to recruit within each county. Thus the character of Flash and Trim and the methods they employ probably reflect upon the Committee. To Munford, who remained in charge of all military matters in his county, this irregularity of conflicting responsibilities must have seemed unnecessary and even foolish.

The manner in which Munford has interwoven his three plots—the burlesque Strut-Isabella plot, the farcical Pickle-Melinda plot, and the principal Trueman-Mira plot—shows an amazing dramatic talent. Not only is unity promoted by relationships between the characters themselves and the Committee, but variety and continuity are achieved by a pattern of alternation which Munford evidently learned by studying and viewing the traditional type of comedy. Here even the best comic dramatists, like Vanbrugh or even Sheridan, sometimes dwelt too long upon one of their plots or finished one of them too early in the play. The serious scenes which develop the theme but do not at first seem to advance the plot are placed in Acts II and IV, where they do not impede empathy with the characters too early or end the drama on too serious a note. Scenes which advance the action of each of the three plots occur in at least four of the five acts. All the plots are started in Act I, and only the burlesque plot is completed before Act V—in the last scene of Act IV. Along with the alternation of martial and romantic songs which Munford provided for his characters, these alternations keep all the plots moving and provide a pleasing variety of the type which the audience evidently relished. With their lyric, farcical, and comic elements admixed, the romantic plots serve to give a variety of suspense, romance, and humor to the play.

All of these plots involve also the basic theme of loyalty. The agency which is at first seen as defining and enforcing this loyalty, as well as providing soldiers to fight for it, is the County Committee.

Few records of the Mecklenburg Committee have survived except the rare communications to the Virginia *Gazette;* but if one can judge from the records of the county court, which are uninterrupted, the extremists in Mecklenburg County must have decided to infiltrate the court as well as to utilize separate jurisdiction. John Speed, Committee chairman, was second in rank to Munford on the court; and in Munford's absence he seems to have operated the court as a sort of legally constituted Committee.

Although Munford, like any other artist, was universalizing the issue of loyalty rather than reproducing on stage the personalities and actions of a group of Southside Virginians, some members of the Committee as presented in *The Patriots* have recognizable originals.

The presiding officer, Colonel Simple, is represented as a

rather ineffective, senile gentleman who has just resigned his commission, having decided it "best to decline in time" (p. 75) and leave military prestige and command for younger men. Oddly enough in the cast of characters he is not grouped with the members of the Committee. Probably Colonel Simple is a caricature of Henry Deloney, who in 1766 and 1767 represented Mecklenburg in the House of Burgesses and who sat on the county court for years as the third ranking member. When the Mecklenburg Committee was elected, he was passed over, possibly because he was inadequately militant. Deloney actually presided when the Scots were tried in Mecklenburg Court. Like Colonel Simple, moreover, he declined in time. On 8 September 1777, with Munford briefly present in court, Deloney was nominated for a colonelcy in the Mecklenburg militia; on 13 October, however, when he and Munford were both present. Deloney's name was omitted from the suggested muster of officers.[23] Henry Deloney's son, Henry, Jr., signed the petition against the Scots; the father, whose counterpart Colonel Simple displays little animus against the Scots, did not.[24]

Among the Committee members Colonel Strut had become a delegate to win his Isabella; the other delegate, Mr. Summons, to acquire wealth.

> *Sum.* . . . When I became a delegate, I was told it was the ready way to some profitable post. I long to serve my country.
> *True.* Enter into the army, sir; that is the way to preferment.
> *Sum.* I am a cripple, and can't be a soldier.
> *Mean.* Be a colonel of militia then, 'tis a fine post for cripples, for they never march, but they have no pay, Mr. Summons: you want a post that will bring you something. (p. 70)

Probably Mr. Summons is a satirical portrait of Joseph Speed, the other delegate from Mecklenburg County. Speed kept an inn at his father's home. As Mira points out concerning militia captains, there "are so many . . . now-a-days" (p. 62), yet even as late as 1777 Joseph Speed seems to have held no rank in the militia. He had been elected to the Committee. The appellation "Mr. Summons" is timely and appropriate: on 8 April 1776 he resigned his post as undersheriff to accept the position as delegate.[25] Doubtless there are hints of other Speeds in the portrait, for the post of "Mr. Summon"s seems to have gone to the Speeds almost as a family prerogative. All six of the boys—John Jr., James, Henry, Lewis, Joseph, and Matthew—held the post of undersheriff at one time or another; five of them were appointed to the post by their father when he took the oath of office as sheriff in 1767.[26] Joseph had actually been appointed 8 July 1765, when he was fifteen.[27] The father served as sheriff for several terms.

One other member of the Committee may be in part a caricature. Thunderbolt, a military-minded militia officer whose lieutenant strips Flash in a game of all-fours, may perhaps be a takeoff on Thacker Burwell, a member of the local Committee. Brazen, as has been pointed out, had his character dictated by his role and probably suggests no local counterpart. Squib and Skip are merely echoing voices needed to bring the Committee to full strength, too vague to suggest contemporary originals, although Skip's name was probably taken from the role Sir Peyton Shipwith ("Skipper") played on the Committee.

Although one can identify the originals of several of the members of the Committee in *The Patriots*, Munford is satirizing not so much the particular actions of the Mecklenburg Committee, which evidently acted far less than did other Committees, as some of the abuses, the extremes to which the Committees went all over Virginia and all over the other Colonies. According to Eckenrode, "County committees, indeed, sometimes showed a small intolerance, an inquisitorial, and perhaps tyrannical, spirit. . . ."[28] This judgment recalls Meanwell's comment upon the treatment of the Scots: "our holy inquisition are for the very moderate correction the Jews received in Spain" (p. 69).

The county Committees composed the quite necessary force which at first provided for troops and munitions and at the same time attacked the suspected Fifth Column of Scots and other loyalists. At first these committees functioned more or less independently, but from 17 August 1775, their work was correlated by the central committee of Safety. By the summer of that year they existed in more than thirty counties.[29] Despite their extra-legality they were elected in the traditional manner by the free-holders of the county and included competent and respected local leaders. In adjoining Charlotte County, for example, the Committee was headed by Paul Carrington.

Punishment meted out by these committees for disloyalty had gradually become more severe. In December of 1775 punishment by public announcement—entailing disgrace and boycott—was made more severe; it became sequestration of property and a prison term, and five members of each local committee were empowered to conduct a trial for loyalism.[30] In May of 1776 the punishment became forfeiture of property and an indefinite prison term. The committees were given now the additional responsibility of administering a loyalty oath to all suspected persons; and refusal to take

this oath was punished, as it is in *The Patriots,* by the seizure
of arms and ammunition.[31] Later in the year sterner measures were
directed against dissent or criticism of the state.[32]

In August of 1777, however, as has been seen, the functions
of the local committees were actually turned over to the revived
county courts, which in Mecklenburg County had been meeting
and acting right along without proper legal jurisdiction.[33] When
the responsibility of administering the oath to all males over sixteen
became in May of 1777 fixed upon the county courts, Munford
found himself, on 14 July 1777, saddled with the disagreeable
personal responsibility of administering the oath within his own
district.[34] No doubt his intense feelings upon such a duty helped
to give rise to *The Patriots,* for it is this problem of loyalty which
provides the central experience and the central theme of the play.

The Committee is concerned especially with disloyalty among
the Scottish merchants and the suspected tories. Toward neither
group does it display much understanding or toleration. When the
members of the Committee meet to discuss the Scots, they reach
their decision quickly:

Braz. How goes it? How goes it? Well, what business do we meet
upon to-day?
Strut. The Scabbies are to be tried according to the ordinance.
Bra. Let's duck the scoundrels.
Thun. Duck 'em! let's burn the scoundrels.
Skip. Let's hang them.
Squib. Ay, ay, hang them, that is the best way. (p. 71)

Pleas of innocence and demand for proof of guilt do little good:
"Proof, sir!" Brazen replies, "we have proof enough. We suspect
any Scotchman: suspicion is proof, sir. I move for the question,
Mr. President" (p. 73).

Munford's own tolerant attitude is voiced by his hero Meanwell:

The ungracious treatment that some Scotchmen have met with,
the illiberal reflections cast out against them all, give little hope of
their attachment to a country, or to a people, where and with whom
they have already tasted the bitter herb of persecution: some there
are, who have behaved well, conform'd to the public will, nor given
any cause of offense; yet even those have not met with the common
offices of civility among us. (p. 69)

Some of Munford's closest ties were Scottish. After his father's
death, his mother had married a Scot; and Currie had evidently
been kind and generous to his stepson. Another Scot, Archibald
McRobert, had married Munford's only sister, Elizabeth, and was

a leading figure in his county in organizing early resistance to the English. Munford's own pastor, John Cameron, was so able that Munford entrusted to him the education of his son, William; and indeed an anecdote about Cameron may have furnished a hint for a crude, farcical related incident in the play. Stitch, doorkeeper to the Committee, reports how Mr. Preachwell received his summons for eating on a fast day:

The parson snuff'd up his nose as bad as if he smell'd a stink. I'm sartin, says I, it's not me that has let a ——, mentioning the thing itself, an't like your honour. The words were hardly out of my mouth, before spang he took me with his foot.
  Sim. The parson strike!
  Stitch. Yes; look, your honour, just here an't please your honour. (*shewing his b—k si-e.*)
  Sim. Praise be to God, our holy teachers detest fighting.
  Stitch. I said so, an't please your honour. You a parson, says I! By jing, he ran at me as vigue-rous as a lion, with a monstratious stick; but durn the heels, thinks I, that lets the body suffer; so off I ran. (pp. 100-101)

Cameron, it will be recalled from petitions submitted by the parishioners of St. James, was evidently quite unpopular with a sizeable and vocal part of the Mecklenburgers. Stitch's account indeed may have been adapted from an earlier incident involving the Scots in general and Cameron in particular, as reported on 22 December 1774: "Nothing going on here but Associations & Committees, though they are not so violent against the *Scotch* as with you. I was lately in Mecklenburg, in Virginia, where one Malachi Macalle was carrying about a paper for expelling out of the country all *Scotchmen*, to which he had got 300 names. However, for his ill-bred invections against that country in general & against some individuals in particular, the Parson of the Parish (one Cameron from the Highlands) followed him and gave him a good & most complete caning."[35]

The three Scots who appear on trial in the play, McFlint, McGripe, and McSqueeze, are basically merely farcical figures. They are differentiated by the conventional English and the willingness of one of the three to temporize and the Scottish dialect and the loyalty of the other two to the Mother Country. McFlint alleges that he was bred in Scotland, but not born there:

  McSqueeze. What, Sandy, do you deny your country mon, tak shame to yoursel, Sandy.
  McFlint. It is time to deny man, when they make it a crime to be born there. (pp. 73-74)

But the trial itself probably utilizes to some extent the trial of the Scottish merchants before the Mecklenburg Court on 14 April 1777. At that time Thomas Banks, William Turnbull, John Johnson, John Brown, and Ebenezer McHarg, all Scottish or British factors or storekeepers for British merchants, were tried and declared within the resolution; and William Duncan, Adam Newell, and William McClure were added to the list.[36] Another, James McCan, was on 8 September 1777 cited by the Court for "tending to excite Tumults and disorders in the State."[37] At the general trial only McHarg appeared. He was obviously an original for McFlint. A factor for Alexander Donald and Co., he had lived in Mecklenburg County for some twenty years, and his brother Alexander and he had doubtless made many enemies by the almost countless lawsuits they had instituted on behalf of Donald and Co. Since he had been so long a resident and had married a Virginian he successfully petitioned the House of Delegates to be allowed to take the required oath; and on 15 November 1779 it was decided that he should be considered a citizen of the Commonwealth.[38]

Animus against the Scots in Mecklenburg County and McHarg, in particular, was widespread. Exactly a month after the trial, a petition from Mecklenburg County was presented to the Speaker of the House of Delegates, requesting,

the resolution respecting the Factors of British merchants extended to the married, as well as the single natives of Great Britain, who were factors for, or partners with, merchants residing in Great Britain, and have not uniformly manifested a friendly disposition to the American cause; and who notwithstanding their Connexion in this Country by Marriage, declare that the paper currency of this State, now in circulation, is of very little value, or no value, and absolutely refuse to receive the same, in discharge of the debts due to the British merchants. . . . Wherefore your Petitioners pray that all the natives of Great Britain, who have not uniformly shown their friendly disposition to the American cause, may be compelled to leave this state. And that some more severe punishment may be inflicted upon those who depreciate the paper currency. . . .[39]

Among the 189 signers of this petition were Bennett Goode, Isaac Holmes, Henry Deloney, Jr., Joseph Goode, Jr., and Sir Peyton Skipwith. Munford did not sign.

But the unfair treatment of the Scots, for which Munford is using particularly Mecklenburg materials with which he was familiar, characterized Mecklenburg County no more than other Virginia counties, or other states. In Virginia as a whole the attitude toward the Scots was at first rather lenient; even as late as

December, 1775, after the war had really begun in earnest, the prejudice against the Scots was still opposed.[40] But with the formation
of the various Committees of Observation, the attitude toward them
began to harden. On 18 December 1776 the House of Delegates
adopted a resolution to expel all British merchants, instructing the
Governor to enforce the law which provided that all "natives of
Great Britain who are partners with agents, storekeepers, assistant
storekeepers, or clerks for any merchant in Great Britain—except
only such as heretofore uniformly manifested a friendly disposition
to this country by having wives or children here" should depart
within forty days.[41] Otherwise they were to be considered enemies.
This resolution, ironically enough, became effective on 1 January
1777, which brought also news of Byrd's suicide and the glorious
American victory at Trenton.

The county court, rather than the county Committee of Observation, was directed to enforce these laws against the Scots, and
in Mecklenburg County the court duly reviewed and reported
names to the Council. Munford has transferred to the Committee
a scene which would have actually occurred at the time dramatized,
and used a scene which in Mecklenburg County did so occur, in
Court. Obviously Munford wanted to throw upon the Committees,
rather than the regular courts, the full responsibilities of prosecution.

But the more important group of those suspected of disloyalty
are those accused of being tories. The hero Trueman objects to the
loose use of the term *tory* to brand any nonconformity:

> *True.* Explain what you mean by the word tory, gentlemen.
> *Sim.* Tory! why surely every body knows what a tory is—a tory
> is—pray, gentlemen, explain to him what a tory is.
> *Strut.* A tory, sir, is any one who disapproves of men and measures.
> *Braz.* All suspected persons are call'd tories.
> *True.* If suspicion makes a tory, I may be one; if a disapprobation
> of men and measures constitutes a tory, I am one; but if a real attach-
> ment to the true interests of my country stamps me her friend, then
> I detest the opprobrious epithet of tory, as much as I do the inflama-
> tory distinction of whig. (p. 104)

The central theme of the play seems stated and the plot adum-
brated in the early discussion between Trueman and Meanwell:

> *Mean.* What a pity it is that all heads are not capable of re-
> ceiving the benign influence of the principles of liberty—some are
> too weak to bear it, and become thoroughly intoxicated. The cause
> of my country appears as dear to me as to those who most passionately
> declaim on the subject. The rays of the sun of freedom, which is
> now rising, have warmed my heart; but I hope my zeal against

tyranny will not be shown by bawling against it, but by serving my country against her enemies; and never may I signalize my attachment to liberty by persecuting innocent men, only because they differ in opinion with me.

True. It seems for this very reason you are not accounted a patriot; but truth will at last prevail, the faithful heart be applauded, and the noisy hypocrite stripped of the mask of patriotism.

Mean. I hope so; and therefore truth, plain truth, shall be the only shield I will use against my foes. Men who aim at power without merit, must conceal the meanness of their souls by noisy and passionate speeches in favour of every thing which is the current opinion of the day; but real patriots are mild, and secretly anxious for their country, but modest in expressions of zeal. They are industrious in the public service, but claim no glory to themselves. (p. 57)

In the plot Munford uses ridicule to expose false patriotism and encourage true and moderate patriotism by the conduct of his principal hero and heroine. The virulent patriotism of Isabella is discredited, as is the pretended patriotism of Tackabout, who lodges information with the Committee against Meanwell and Trueman. His tergiversation discredits his accusations, and he is eventually uncased as a tory himself. When the Committee turn upon Tackabout in anger, Munford manages to dissolve their animus into laughter in a manner befitting comedy, and Tackabout is booted from the courthouse by the hero.

The tory Tackabout is particularized with several details. He explains his reluctance to take a commission on the strength of "some expectations in England; the reversion of a considerable estate, or—";

Bra. Poh! damn the estate; let it go.

Tack. My ancestors lost an estate by their loyalty; I should not choose to lose mine by my disloyalty.

Sim. 'Tis a sin to lose an estate any how, that's certain.

Tack. A man's patrimony, in my opinion, is a sacred depositum, especially when an expected title gives lustre to the possession. (pp. 75-76)

These comments and Tackabout's activities seem to point clearly to Sir Peyton Skipwith, seventh baronet of the title and Munford's neighbor in Mecklenburg County. The Cavalier founder of the line, Sir Henry Skipwith, had actually had to sell his English estate, Prestwould, probably at a heavy loss, in 1653; and his younger son, Sir Grey, third baronet Skipwith, had come to Virginia.[42] Sir Peyton himself, seventh baronet Skipwith, had for several years served on the county commission and had been elected to the committee. As sheriff of Mecklenburg County during 1777 he would naturally be concerned with disloyalty in the county.[43] He signed the petition against the Scots, and his name is notably absent from the lists of militia officers, quite differently from his younger brother Colonel Henry Skipwith, who led Munford's regiment in the battle of Guildford Court House.

Suddenly on 13 July 1778 Skipwith was returned no inhabitant of the county.[44] Then, on 4 June 1781, Sir Peyton was actually tried in Mecklenburg Court for treasonable correspondence with the enemy. He was found innocent by a court presided over by Munford himself.[45] The identification of Sir Peyton as the probable original of Tackabout is strengthened by the fact that Sabine gives a brief biography of Sir Peyton as a loyalist and the fact that his eldest son, Grey, actually returned to England and reestablished the line there.[46] This indentification also strengthens the supposition that the play was completed before Camden. Surely Munford would not have written the play as late as 1781, when the actual trial would have made the identification serious; and the marriage of his own daughter Elizabeth to Richard Kennon, nephew to Sir Peyton, allied the two families.

Very little suppression of the freedom of speech seems to have been occasioned by the Mecklenburg court. On 14 September 1778 John Cardin was summoned to appear at court for "speaking disrespectfully of the measures of this Commonwealth." Not until 10 May 1779 did the trial actually take place. Then Cardin was found guilty by a jury of twelve men, fixed £5 costs, and jailed for forty-eight hours.[47] More than a year later, Leonard Cardin was charged with having harbored two deserters from the Southern Service, but on 9 October 1780 the case was dismissed.[48] These were the cases of disloyalty tried in the Mecklenburg court.

Thus the major local material here was not actual oppression, but the coldness with which some Mecklenburgers treated Munford because of his friends and relatives, some of whom were strongly suspected, and his own feelings when he was called upon to take and administer the loyalty oath. Indeed Munford was, perhaps unconsciously, mirroring somewhat his own feelings and experience in the part of George Worthy's uncle, the bachelor Meanwell. Though a disinterested friend of man and of his country, Meanwell, evidently like Munford himself, is in 1777 still suspected as not zealous enough in his country's behalf. Munford probably suffered no personal examination by the Committee, but he felt the oppression which many Virginians and other colonists of good will felt because of intolerance. Especially did he appreciate the plight of his brother-in-law Robert Beverley, whose very name came to be joined to that of tory and who was disarmed as such by the Committee of Essex.[49] Beverley was notoriously cool toward the Revolution, and during the war his sympathies with the Mother Country were strong. Although he blamed Lord North and the Parliament for American discontent, he tried to remain uncommitted: "I profess myself to be a Man of no Party," he wrote.[50] To his brother-in-law William Fitzhugh he confided on 20 July 1775, "I am conscious of the Rectitude of my own Intentions & let the Temper of the Times be even more dangerous than they are, my Conscience shall be my guide." He went on to notice that "by some strange Metamorphosis or other, this Contrariety of Opinions is denied."[51] Doubtless he wrote in the same strain to Munford. Relationships between the two families were always close. One of the Beverley sons was named Munford, and a daughter was named Anna Munford. Munford named his elder daughter Elizabeth Beverley. The other two men who married Beverley sisters, William Fitzhugh of Marmion, and James Mills, wealthy merchant of Urbanna, were likewise cool towards the Revolution. More than merely cool was of course William Byrd III, one of Munford's earliest and closest friends, to whom in 1775 he had promised to do what he could to help maintain ties of loyalty with England. Byrd's suicide on 1 January 1777 doubtless affected Munford strongly, and news of the victory at Trenton did not dispel the gloom.

But the essential examination in *The Patriots* is far more universal than the caricature of Mecklenburg patriots acting in committee, far more universal than the persecution of Scottish merchants or Virginia moderators or loyalists during the Revolution. The play dramatizes an aspect of a particularly American problem; thus when it was first analyzed, the critic Seilhamer, not knowing the author, did not venture to identify the locale as Virginia. Although it is indeed universal, it is nowhere more pressing than in our nation of many minorities. In a time of war or its aftermath suspicion is always concentrated upon the minorities— upon the Scots in the Revolution, upon German descendants during World War I, upon the American Nipponese in World War II. And suspicion likewise is attached to those who voice sympathy with these minorities, or those who are not adequately violent in their denunciations, as upon anyone of even mildly leftist sympathies during and after World War II while McCarthyism was at its height of frenzy. The odium is always attached in war time or time of crisis to one who, like Munford, insists upon retaining complete human dignity. Placed in such a position that he was able to understand and appreciate conflicting ideals and loyalties, Munford was for a time judged guilty by association and guilty because he expressed no immoderate hatreds. In his play, however, he was able to speak dramatically, sincerely, and ably of a problem which even now remains an inconsistency of the American way.

~~~ VII ~~~

Epilogue: Rediscovery

SETTING an example of filial piety which was to be followed in turn by his own sons, William Munford in 1798 edited *A Collection of Plays and Poems, by the late Col. Robert Munford, of Mecklenburg County, in the State of Virginia.* Born in 1775, William began to publish as early as 1792, and he was even then planning to bring out a volume of his own and his father's plays and poems. Writing to his friend John Coalter on 17 May 1792, he remarked, "The poem I mentioned in my last [on the defeat of General St. Clair] has been printed, and the copies of the first impression being almost sold . . . I intend to employ another printer in the fall to publish it again, together with all my father's poems, &c. This work, I shall bring into the world with a subscription."[1] Evidently he failed to secure enough signatures; and unfortunately the family finances were so involved and straitened that until 1798 he could not afford to subsidize publication. Then he unfortunately selected as his publisher William Prentis, a Petersburg printer whose scope was generally limited to the semiweekly *Virginia Gazette and Petersburg Intelligencer*, a yearly Virginia almanac, and an occasional volume of local political interest.[2] Although he had only the year before published proposals for printing the poems of Gavin Turnbull, no copy exists, and probably the project was never realized.[3] The Munford volume was thus probably his first venture into creative literature, and he evidently had inadequate publishing connections to distribute the book nationally. In effect, the book was hardly published by Prentis in the sense in which we now understand the term; it was rather printed and sold by him at the expense of the editor, William Munford.

For half a century the very existence of Robert Munford's plays was unknown to scholars of American literature. When in 1889 *The Patriots* was finally discovered and described, it was read in a fragment which failed to reveal its authorship. Moreover, the same copy created bibliographical problems by raising a ghost which has not yet been laid.

Like William's own volume, published the same year in Richmond, *A Collection* attracted little and only local attention. A third of a century later, in the rich bibliography which William Dunlap appended to his *History of the American Theatre* (1832), he did not mention the volume. The same year in which Dunlap published his book in New York, the Library Company of Philadelphia acquired what was evidently the first copy secured by a public or university library.[4] Unfortunately it was a defective copy consisting only of the two plays, bound in a miscellaneous volume of drama which comprised A. von Kotzebue's *La Peyrouse*, the 1800 edition published in New York; the then anonymous (John Leacock's) *The Fall of British Tyranny, or American Liberty Triumphant* (Philadelphia, 1776); John Murdock's *The Politicians* (Philadelphia, 1798); Munford's two plays, *The Candidates* credited to William Munford and *The Patriots* anonymous, both assigned to Philadelphia as the place of publication; and finally William Macready's *The Bank Note* (London, 1746).[5] The plays which immediately preceded Munford's in the volume were published in Philadelphia. Plausible therefore was the cataloguer's mistake in assigning to Philadelphia Munford's plays. Evidently some time before James Cox acquired the Munford plays, in 1808,[6] the general title page and most of William Munford's Preface had been torn away, and when the various plays were bound together, William Munford's signature at the end of the Preface was mistakenly assumed to indicate authorship. Perhaps there is some other explanation of the mistaken attribution, for on the very page (p. vii) signed by William Munford occurs the comment: "The author intended, if he had lived, to translate the whole work [*Metamorphoses*], but death put an end to his design." At any rate, whoever bound the plays must have removed whatever preliminary leaves then remained preceding the separate title page for *The Candidates*. Although the pagination was continuous for the two plays, there was no running title to indicate common authorship, and a librarian cataloging the plays in such a miscellaneous volume might easily be forgiven for hesitating to assign *The Patriots* to William Munford. But the cataloguer was evidently the only one who examined the plays. It was half a century before a literary historian called for, read, and described either play.

Finally, in 1846, the filial piety of William's own sons indirectly aroused some interest in Robert Munford. At the time of his death, in 1825, William Munford had just completed a translation of Homer's *Iliad*. His death delayed publication for more than twenty years, but in 1846 his widow and sons brought out a handsome edition in New York.[7] It contained itself no reference to the translator's father. But among the reviews of the translation, all of them published that same year, three of the reviewers prefaced their criticisms with a brief biography of the translator and at least mentioned his parents. By Nathaniel Beverley Tucker, writing in *The Southern Literary Messenger*, Robert was not even named, William being "the only son of a gentleman of considerable landed estate in Virginia."[8] The irony here is that Tucker was a Munford cousin and that he may already have acquired the Tucker-Coleman copy of the plays.[9] In his article in the *North American Review*, Longfellow's friend Cornelius Conway Felton gave considerable praise to Anna Beverley Munford, but Robert Munford was merely "a distinguished patriot" who "died, when William was only eight years old."[10] Only George F. Holmes, writing in *The Southern Quarterly Review* and employing there "materials furnished by two distinguished gentlemen who were intimately acquainted with" William, mentioned the father's literary interests. After naming Robert Munford and commenting that some of William's ancestors had signalized themselves in the Revolution, he added that the father "is represented as having been a gentleman of considerable attainments, fond of letters, and noted for his fond and active patriotism."[11] Nowhere in the reviews, then, was there any indication that Robert Munford had ever written anything.

But in *The Southern Literary Messenger* Tucker employed some acid comments taking to task Northern anthologists in general and Rufus Wilmot Griswold in particular for their neglect of superior Southern performances in favor of minor Yankee productions. Tucker in effect accused Griswold of operating his anthologies like a closed corporation. The accusation got results. Griswold not only inserted in the later editions of his *Poets and Poetry of America* a fairly detailed account of William Munford, but he also began the article with a brief notice of the father, Robert Munford:

His father, Colonel ROBERT MUNFORD, was honourably distinguished in affairs during the Revolution, and afterward gave much attention to literature. Some of his letters, to be found in collections relating to the time, are written with grace and vigour, and he was the author of several dramatic pieces, of considerable merit, which, with a few minor poems, were published by his son, the subject of the present article, at Petersburg, in 1798. In his best comedy, "The Candidates," in three acts, he exposes to contempt the falsehood and corruption by which it was frequently attempted to influence the elections. In "The Patriots," in five acts, he contrasts, probably with an eye to some instance in Virginia, a real and pretended love of country. He had commenced a translation of Ovid's "Metamorphoses" into English verse, and had finished the first book, when death arrested his labours. He was a man of wit and humour, and was respected for many social virtues. His literary activity is referred to thus particularly, because I have not seen that the pursuits and character of the father, have been noticed by any of the writers upon the life of the son, which was undoubtedly in a very large degree influenced by them.

Griswold's notice was summarized in the *Cyclopaedia of American Literature*, published in 1856 by Evert A. and George Duyckinck.[13] From this time, Robert Munford became an item in the biographical dictionaries. But for the rest of the century what Griswold printed evidently remained the sum total of knowledge available about Robert Munford. The plays themselves were not then available; only the imperfect copy in the Philadelphia Library Company was then known, and it had not been properly identified. Additional copies gradually found their places on shelves of the great libraries. In 1869 the Library Company of Philadelphia acquired a second and perfect copy of *The Collection of Plays and Poems*, the James Rush copy;[14] and also about this time the Library of Congress received the Pleasants copy, the first of three which at one time it was to possess.[15] In 1873 the Boston Public Library acquired the Thomas Pennant Barton copy.[16] Unfortunately before these volumes reached their destined shelves, Joseph Sabin had completed his collections and was arranging material for his great *Bibliotheca Americana*. By the time he reached the volume in which Robert Munford should have finally made his appearance, in 1880, two perfect copies were easily accessible, but he had completed his collections in 1864,[17] at which time only the imperfect Philadelphia copy was known. In 1884, then, using the 1835 Philadelphia *Catalogue*, he gave as number 59092, under its title, the anonymous listing "The Patriots. A Comedy in Five Acts. *Philadelphia*. [n.d.] 8 vo." For some reason he ignored *The Candidates*.[18]

Five years later, in his *History of the American Theatre*, George O. Seilhamer finally provided an analysis of *The Patriots*. By this time still another copy had come into a large library: in 1884 Brown University had acquired the Thomas H. Ellis-Harriss copy.[19] But by some incredible mischance or oversight Seilhamer in Philadelphia read the fragmentary Cox copy rather than the complete Rush copy. Thus the play continued to remain anonymous and Munford continued to remain unknown even though historians of American drama had for the first time an analysis of the plot, some indication of the characters and themes, and even samples of the dialogue.[20] In his voluminous two volume *Literary History of the American Revolution* (New York, (1897) Moses Coit Tyler wrote nothing of Munford.

Even though Robert Munford was recognized by the biographical dictionaries as the author of *The Candidates* and *The Patriots*, scholars continued to label as anonymous the "Philadelphia" *Patriots* described by Seilhamer. In 1900 and again in 1905, Oscar Wegelin listed by name the plays of Robert Munford and listed as anonymous the "Philadelphia" *Patriots*, by now a healthy ghost with a habitat conferred by the 1835 Philadelphia *Catalogue* and confirmed by Sabin, Seilhamer, and Wegelin. Only in his Index did Wegelin accidentally bring together the author and the ghost edition, though by 1905 he could have easily consulted at least four complete copies, and in 1905 Wegelin actually added the information that Munford's *Collection* comprised 206 pages.[21]

But if one becomes irritated with Northern historians and bibliographers for their failure to make an obvious identification, in Virginia scholars were not doing much for their native son. In 1895 Louise Manly in her *Southern Literature* recorded only Munford's name and the titles of his plays; and in his 1900 doctoral dissertation at the University of Virginia Sidney Ernest Bradshaw, ignoring the richer materials he could have found in his 1852 edition of Griswold, added only the scanty information about Munford gathered from biographical dictionaries—and probably added another Munford ghost: William Munford, he said, had printed an edition of his father's *Collection* in 1798 at Richmond as well as at Petersburg.[22] Although in the Virginia historical and genealogical magazines his name occurred several times, it was to record his lineage or his services in the legislature. Before the 1920's he was named there as an author only once, by Lyon G. Tyler, in 1898, as "Robert Munford, author of Munford's *Poems*."[23] In his *History of Southern Literature* (1906), Carl Holliday, of the University of Virginia, added nothing to Miss Manly's information. Perhaps one should not judge these Virginia scholars too severely. The University has evidently never owned a copy of the *Collection*. The State Library is uncertain when it acquired its copy; and the only other Southern copy found, apart from Mrs. Mary Haldane Coleman's, came to the University of Richmond in the winter of 1944-1945.[24]

With the increased availability of copies one would have supposed that this ignorance of Munford would soon be dispelled.[25] But ignorance was compounded with confusion. In his *Literature of the South* (1910) Montrose J. Moses supplied a few details about Munford's *Candidates*.[26] But in 1925 in his *The American Dramatist*, he attributed *The Patriots* to Col. William Munford.[27] Even worse, because the work remains standard, Arthur Hobson Quinn in 1923 endowed the "Philadelphia" ghost *Patriots* with a birthdate to match the birthplace. Perhaps using the 1835 Philadelphia *Catalogue* and inadvertently picking up the date "1776" from the line immediately above the *Patriots* entry, he announced 1776 as the date of publication of a ghost edition, confirmed the date in 1951;[28] and the date has been accepted ever since. The way in which the mistake probably arose has been explained; the librarians at the Philadelphia Library Company assure us that the copy described as the "Philadelphia" edition is in fact only a section of the 1798 Petersburg edition.[29] The date 1776 is manifestly absurd; no play published in 1776 could have predicted the battles of Princeton and Trenton unless the author was either blessed with extraordinary good luck or such extrasensory perception that he was surely the proper father to such a ghost.

But as one ghost is laid to rest, another is being created. In *Three Centuries of Drama: American*, edited by Mr. Henry W. Wells, the Recordax Company in its 1953 microprint edition of *The Candidates* and *The Patriots* has created a new, 1792 ghost. Since Mr. Wells used the Pleasants copy in the Library of Congress and the copy in the American Antiquarian Society, both of which are the 1798 edition,[30] the 1792 date is obviously incorrect. But when scholars get hold of William Munford's letter of 17 May 1792, promising John Coalter to bring out an edition of his father's works later that year,[31] it may take another century to lay this young "1792" ghost. Indeed errors about Munford and his plays flourish so vigorously that at times one despairs. For example, in the widely adopted textbook *The Literature of the South*, the editors tell us, "Colonel Robert Munford wrote *The Candidates; or The Humours of a Virginia Election* in Petersburg in 1798."[32] Ghost writing indeed: Munford had died in 1783.

Notes

CHAPTER I

1. Thomas Jefferson to William Wirt, 5 August 1815, in Thomas Jefferson, *The Writings of Thomas Jefferson*, ed. Lipscomb (Washington, 1903-1904), XIV, 338.

2. Beverley Bland Munford, *Random Recollections* (New York, 1905), p. 215; John Smith, *The General Historie of Virginia, New England & the Summer Isles* (Glasgow, 1907), I, 124, 263; "Mumford and Munford," *William and Mary Quarterly*, First Series, XI (1902-1903), 75.

3. Philip Slaughter, *A History of Bristol Parish, Virginia*, 2d. ed. (Richmond, 1879), p. 194 n.

4. Albert S. Borgman, *The Life and Death of William Mountfort* (Cambridge, Mass., 1935).

5. "Mumford and Munford Families," *Tyler's Quarterly Historical and Genealogical Magazine*, III (1921-1922), 174.

6. Charles City County, *Charles City County Court Orders*, abstracted by Beverley Fleet, in *Virginia Colonial Abstracts* (Baltimore, 1961), X, 11; XIII, 33.

7. The marriage license was registered 22 December 1701 (Henrico County Deeds, 1697-1704, p. 279). In this biography dates of the month have been retained in Old Style, but the year has been regularized to New Style.

8. For example, see the record of 9 July 1706 of Perquimans Precinct Court, North Carolina, in North Carolina, *North Carolina Colonial Records*, I, ed. William L. Saunders (Raleigh, 1886), 652.

9. William Byrd II, *Secret Diary of William Byrd of Westover, 1709-1712*, ed. Louis B. Wright and Marion Tinling (Richmond, 1941), passim.

10. Byrd, *A Journey to the Land of Eden, Anno 1733*, in *The Prose Works of William Byrd of Westover*, ed, Louis B. Wright (Cambridge: Harvard University Press, 1966), pp. 411-412.

11. *Ibid.*, p. 384.

12. *Ibid.*, p. 408.

13. Byrd, *Secret Diary*, pp. 11, 32, 36, 44.

14. Prince George County Orders, 1714-1720, pp. 19, 95; Bristol Parish, *The Vestry Book and Register of Bristol Parish, Virginia, 1720-1789*, ed. Churchill Gibson Chamberlayne (Richmond, 1898), p. 7 and passim.

15. *Ibid.*, p. 75.

16. Byrd, *Another Secret Diary of William Byrd of Westover, 1739-1741*, ed. Maude Woodfin and Marion Tinling (Richmond, 1942), p. 30.

17. Bristol Parish. *Vestry Book*, p. 83.

18. Virginia, Council, *Journals of the Council of Virginia in Executive Sessions, 1737-1763*, in *The Virginia Magazine of History and Biography*, XV (1907-1908), 235-236.

19. William Beverley to Richard Bland, "Some Letters of William Beverley," ed. Worthington Chauncey Ford, in *William and Mary Quarterly*, First Series,

III (1894-1895), 233, corrected by the writer from a microfilm copy in the Virginia State Library of the original in the New York Public Library.

20. Mrs. Elizabeth Beverley to Capt. Theoderick Bland, Sr., 26 July 1745, in the Virginia Historical Society. The letter is printed, with some inaccuracies, in *Va. Mag.*, XXIII (1915), 362.

21. William Beverley to Richard Bennett, 12 February 1745, in "Some Letters of William Beverley," *W. & M.*, 1 Ser., III (1894-1895), 239, corrected by the writer from a positive in the Virginia State Library of the original in the New York Public Library. The mortgage to Theophilus "Feild" was recorded 13 November 1739 in Prince George County Minute Book, 1737-1740, p. 380. Theophilus Field was one of the three executors of the Munford estate (Brunswick County Order Book, III, 4).

22. Hitherto the date of Munford's birth has been invariably and erroneously given as "before 1730." But the date *c.* 1737 is fixed in the lawsuit "Kennon against McRobert and wife." Here it is clearly stated that Robert "was aged about eight years at the time of his father's death" in 1745 (Virginia, Supreme Court of Appeals, *Reports of Cases Argued and Determined in the Court of Appeals of Virginia*, reported by Bushrod Washington [Richmond, 1798-1819], I, 97). The year 1737 may indeed be too early; on 5 September 1759 Matthew Marrable paid for damages to the property of "Munford's orphans" (Lunenburg County Orders, VI, 30 recto). One cannot be certain, however, that Munford had not reached his majority by this time. Local citizens may not have been informed of his actual age, since he was not yet a resident. A garbled account of the McRobert lawsuit, dating his birth at "circa 1727" was published by W. Ronald Cocke, in "Genealogical Notes Gleaned from Virginia Court Reports," *W. & M.*, 2 Ser., XI (1931), 110.

23. Virginia *Gazette*, 3 July 1752, p. 3. On this date it was so described and offered for sale or rent by George Currie. It was later redeemed by the dramatist's mother and sister and in 1770 conveyed to his brother, Theoderick (Kennon against McRobert). After the deaths of the mother and brother it was acquired by Colonel John Banister. British troops under General Phillips rested here before the attack upon Petersburg, according to a letter from Banister to Colonel Theoderick Bland (*The Virginia Historical Register*, IV [1851], 199). According to Edward Wyatt, IV, in *Along Petersburg Streets* (Richmond, 1943), p. 79, it survived severe fighting in the Civil War, became part of Camp Lee, and was razed when that camp was dismantled following World War I. A long avenue shaded by trees still leads to the house site in a clearing surrounded by flowers and shrubs and commanding a distant view of the Appomattox.

24. Some genealogies include also a brother William, allegedly born 28 November 1734, and mistakenly give Elizabeth's birthdate as 1733. But Philip Slaughter, in *A History of Bristol Parish, Va.*, second ed. (Richmond, 1879), p. 133, gives the date of her birth as 27 September 1734 and her baptism as 21 October; and the Bristol Parish *Vestry Book*, p. 340, gives the dates as 22 September 1734 and 21 October.

25. Lunenburg Order Book, I, 227, 281, 314.

26. Most of the details of Munford's education came from William Beverley's 1750 Memorandum Book, deposited with the Beverley Papers in the Virginia Historical Society. Parts of the diary incorporated in this memorandum book were printed by Mr. R. Carter Beverley as "Diary of William Beverley of 'Blandfield' during a Visit to England, 1750," in *Va. Mag.*, XXXVI (1928), 27-35, 161-169. The experiences of some contemporary Virginians at school in England is well delineated in Dr. Lucille Griffith's "English Education for Virginia Youth," *Va. Mag.*, LXIX (1961), 7-27.

27. Matthew Henry Peacock, *History of the Free Grammar School at Wakefield* (Wakefield, 1892), p. 71 and passim.

28. William Munford, Preface, in Robert Munford, *A Collection of Plays and Poems, by the late Colonel Robert Munford, of Mecklenburg, in the State of*

Virginia (Petersburg, 1798), p. vii. The American Antiquarian Society copy, as reproduced in Readex microprint, is always cited.

29. Robert Bolling, of Chellowe, *A Memoir of a Portion of the Bolling Family in England and Virginia*, trans. from the original French by John Robertson, Jr., ed. T. H. Wynne, in *Wynne's Historical Documents from the Old Dominion*, No. IV (Richmond, 1868), pp. 8-9.

30. John McGill, compiler, *The Beverley Family of Virginia* (Columbia, S. C., 1956), p. 535. The will, proved 3 May 1756, was printed in "Will of William Beverley, 1756," *Va. Mag.*, XXII (1914), 297-301.

31. Halifax County Pleas, I, 2, 11, 99; II, 35; *Virginia Gazette*, 16 May 1755, p. 2; "Members of the House of Burgesses," in *Va. Mag.*, VIII (1900-1901), 253.

32. Munford to Theoderick Bland, in the Emmet Collection in New York Public Library. A few conventional contractions have been expanded. A subsequent letter of 23 January 1757 to Uncle Theoderick, now in the Virginia Historical Society, concerns financial trivia. John Banister had married Theoderick Bland's daughter Patsy (Edmund Kimball Alden, "John Banister," in *Dictionary of American Biography*, I, 576).

33. Pages in the contemporary William and Mary "Account Book" covering Theoderick Munford's account are missing.

34. Richard L. Morton, *Colonial Virginia* (Richmond, 1960), II, 686-687.

35. Francis Fauquier to Colonel William Byrd, 19 June 1758, in Virginia, House of Burgesses, *Journals of the House of Burgesses, 1758-1761*, ed. H. R. McIlwaine (Richmond, 1908), pp. 262-263. Subsequent references to the Journals will designate merely *JHB* and include the years of the sessions covered.

36. *The Bland Papers*, ed. Charles Campbell (Petersburg, 1840, 1843), I, 9-10. Brackets are retained for explanatory matter bracketed by Campbell. "Our Col." is Colonel Byrd, not Washington, as mistakenly identified by Campbell and later by Douglas Southall Freeman, *Young Washington* (New York, 1948), II, 389-390. Washington was hardly likely to commend, upon the very day of his arrival, the "conduct hitherto" of a young officer; and a young first lieutenant was hardly likely to dine habitually with the colonel of a rival regiment, but at the table of his own colonel, whose company he probably commanded. Charles Carter, Jr. was the son of Charles Carter of "Cleve," in King George County. By 1756 he was already his father's colleague in the House of Burgesses.

37. Edmund Atkin had been appointed in 1757 King's agent to handle all Indian affairs from Pennsylvania south to Georgia.

38. *Bland Papers*, I, 13-14.

39. George Washington to Henry Bouquet, 18 August 1758, in Henry Bouquet, *The Papers of Col. Henry Bouquet*, ed. Sylvester K. Stevens, *et al.*, (Harrisburg, Pa., 1940, 1951), II, 388; Sinclair to Bouquet, 19 July 1758, in *ibid.*, II, 230; Paul Leicester Ford, *Washington and the Theatre* (New York, 1899), p. 18.

40. According to the affidavit of John Acuff on 27 April 1780 (Henry County Order Book, 1778-1782, II, 85) he "Served as a Serjant under Capt. Robert Munford, in the year 1760, who was under the Command of Colo. Wm. Byrd." But Munford's name does not appear among those of the officers of the Cherokee Campaign of 1760-1761; and in his fruitless attempt to claim bounty from Georgia he made no mention of service beyond the 1758 campaign (Georgia, *The Colonial Records of the State of Georgia*, ed. Allen D. Candler [Atlanta, 1904-1916], X, 175).

CHAPTER II

1. Helpful for the visualization of Munford's Mecklenburg is William B. Hill, ed., *Land by the Roanoke* (Richmond, 1957).

2. Maud Carter Clement, *The History of Pittsylvania County, Virginia* (Lynchburg, 1929), p. 55.

3. *Va. Gaz.*, 4 November 1763, p. 2; Purdie and Dixon *Va. Gaz.*, 26 May 1768, p. 2; Purdie *Va. Gaz.*, 16 May 1766, p. 2; Purdie and Dixon *Va. Gaz.* 16 April 1767, p. 2; Rind *Va. Gaz.*, 9 June 1768, p. 3.

4. Rind *Va. Gaz.*, 15 July 1773, p. 4; Dixon and Hunter *Va. Gaz.*, 25 February 1775, p. 3; Rind *Va. Gaz.*, 28 January 1773, p. 3.

5. Thomas Speed, *Records and Memorials of the Speed Family* (Louisville, 1892), p. 62.

6. Mecklenburg County Order Book, II, 273. Subsequent references will cite this source as MOB.

7. Sketches of Cameron appear in William Meade, *Old Churches, Ministers, and Families of Virginia* (Philadelphia, 1906), I, 485-486, and in Landon C. Bell, *Cumberland Parish, Lunenburg County, Virginia, 1746-1816; Vestry Book, 1746-1816* (Richmond, 1930), pp. 132-165.

8. Judge Sterling Hutcheson, "Richland Hill," in the Clarkesville *Times* and Mecklenburg County *Record*, XII, No. 52 (18 March 1960), p. 1.

9. Robert B. Semple, *A History of the Rise and Progress of the Baptists in Virginia*, rev. G. W. Beale (Richmond, 1894), p. 291.

10. MOB, I, 10.

11. James B. Taylor, *Lives of Virginia Baptist Ministers*, 2nd. ed. (Richmond, 1838), pp. 108-113, 127ff.

12. *JHB, 1770-1772*, pp. 182-183.

13. MOB, III, 283.

14. *JHB, 1770-1772*, pp. 257-258; *JHB, 1773-1776*, p. 80.

15. *Ibid.*, pp. 81, 102-103, 131. On 10 October 1774 William Hunt was brought into court by Matthew Marrable on a charge of breach of peace and had to give security for a year's good behavior (MOB, IV, 292). On 8 August 1774 he had been acquitted on a divided vote in a suit the King vs. William Hunt (MOB, IV, 286).

16. Virginia, House of Delegates, Petitions, 1775-1778, 36, in the Virginia State Library; Virginia, House of Delegates, *Journal of the House of Delegates of Virginia for October, 1779* (Richmond, 1827), p. 10. Subsequent references to these journals will cite *JHD* and designate the session.

17. *JHD, October, 1779*, p. 78. In February of 1781, though probably by Burwell's authority rather than Munford's, John Easter, a Methodist preacher, was drafted in Mecklenburg County for three months' duty (John Frederick Dorman, *Virginia Revolutionary Pension Applications* [Washington, 1958–], VI, 84; *Revolutionary War Records, Mecklenburg County, Virginia*, ed. Katherine B. Elliott [South Hill, Va., 1964], p. 56.)

18. For sketches of McRobert see Joseph Dupuy Eggleston, "Archibald McRobert, Patriot, Scholar, Man of God," (Farmville, n. d.); Herbert Clarence Bradshaw, *History of Prince Edward County, Virginia* (Richmond, 1955), pp. 238-239, 739-740, and passim; and William Meade, I, 448-450, II, 24-26.

19. John Hervey, *Racing in America, 1665-1865*, (New York, 1944), I, 72, 80, 92-93.

20. A convenient survey of racing in Southside Virginia is Nat G. Hutcheson, *What Do You Know about Horses? Mecklenburg County and the Aristocratic Thoroughbreds* (Boydton, Va., n. d.). Additional information is available in Patrick Nisbett Edgar, *The American Race-Turf Register, Sportsman's Herald, and General Stud Book* (New York, 1833), and in Fairfax Harrison, *The Roanoke Stud, 1795-1833* (Richmond, 1930).

21. *The Virginia Gazette, or the American Advertiser*, 2 November 1782.

22. MOB, IV, 332.

23. Lunenburg Order Book, VII, 5 verso.

24. MOB, II, 222.

25. Elizabeth twice dated her birthday in her correspondence with Rachel Mordecai: in letters of 26 April 1818 and 16 February 1821 (from copies made

in 1923 by Mr. E. A. Williams, of Baltimore, and preserved in the Williams family). Since Ursula Anna was married in 1781, she must have been born about 1763.

26. "Will of Robert Beverley, 1756," *Va. Mag.*, XXII (1914), 297-301.

27. Lunenburg, County, *Sunlight on the Southside*, ed. Landon C. Bell (Philadelphia, 1931), p. 255.

28. Virginia Land Grants, Colonial Patents, XXXIII, 794.

29. Lunenburg Deed Book, VI, 390-391.

30. Mecklenburg County Deed Book, I, 394-395; II, 256-257.

31. Virginia, General Assembly, *The Statutes at Large, Being a Collection of All the Laws of Virginia*, ed. W. W. Hening, (Richmond, 1809-1823), X, 124. All subsequent references will cite merely "Hening."

32. A list of livestock sold in 1786, after the war had depleted his herds, shows 41 cows, 16 yearlings, 5 heifers, 28 calves, 22 steers, 6 oxen, and a bull. There was still a herd of 45 sheep (Mecklenburg County Will Book, III, 23-24).

33. "Will of Robert Munford," in *Tyler's Magazine*, XII (1930-31), 89.

34. Bell, *Sunlight*, p. 255.

35. United States, Bureau of the Census, *Heads of Families, Virginia, 1782*, Mecklenburg County, p. 33; Mecklenburg Will Book, III, 18-19.

36. See, for example, *A Collection*, pp. 194-195.

37. Purdie and Dixon *Va. Gaz.*, 16 May 1771, p. 3, Rind *Va. Gaz.*, 23 May 1771, p. 4.

38. Rind *Va. Gaz.*, 12 March 1772, p. 3.

39. Dixon and Hunter *Va. Gaz.*, 16 October 1778, p. 4.

40. Purdie and Dixon *Va. Gaz.*, 2 May 1766, p. 3; MOB, III, 257; Virginia, Council of State, *Journals of the Council of State of Virginia*, ed. H. R. McIlwaine (Richmond, 1931-1932), III, 1596.

41. Sterling Hutcheson, p. 1.

42. Conflicting dimensions are given in two insurance policies: Mutual Assurance Society of Virginia, Vol. XI, policy 176, 6 September 1802; and Vol. XXXVI, policy 342, 24 August 1805 (microfilms in the Virginia State Library). Mecklenburg antiquarians believe that Munford's Richland is not the mansion described in "Kennon Letters," *Va. Mag.*, XXX (1922), 205n.

43. Mecklenburg Will Book, III, 18, 19.

44. Mutual Assurance Society policies cited above and Mecklenburg Will Book, III, 18, 19, 21.

45. All of these she quotes or refers to with familiarity in her correspondence with Rachel Mordecai Lazarus or with her brother Solomon Mordecai.

46. William Munford to Miss Maria Rind, Riveredge (Charles City County), 26 May 1791, in the Coalter correspondence, Library of the College of William and Mary.

47. These straitened accommodations gave rise to a scatalogical poem by a guest, St. George Tucker, in "Robin Hood, a Tale," copied by William Munford in his Miscellany, pp. 88-89, now in the Duke University Library. This poem is not noticed in William Stevens Prince, "St. George Tucker as a Poet of the Early Republic," 1954 Yale doctoral dissertation.

48. Robert Beverley to John Bland (?), summer of 1763, Beverley Letter Book. Library of Congress (microfilm copy in Virginia State Library).

49. Elizabeth Beverley Kennon to Rachel Mordecai Lazarus, 12 May 1822, copy in the Virginia Historical Society.

50. Elizabeth Beverley Kennon to Rachel Mordecai, 10 May 1808, "Some Kennon Letters," *Va. Mag.*, XXXI (1923), 197-198.

51. Cornelius Conway Felton, in *North American Review*, LXIII (1846), 151. Mrs. Munford died when Felton was two years old. He does not indicate his source.

52. Robert Beverley to Robert McKenzie, 1 June 1783, Beverley Letter Book, Library of Congress, from the microfilm in the Virginia State Library.

See also the entry for 13 June 1791 in "Diary of Richard N. Venable, 1791-92," *Tyler's Magazine*, II (1920-1921), 138.

53. MOB, IV, 190.

54. Elizabeth Beverley Kennon to Rachel Mordecai, 8 January 1809, in "Some Kennon Letters," *Va. Mag.*, XXXI (1923), 297.

55. The evidence shows that Robert Munford of Mecklenburg County replaced his stepfather, George Currie, as clerk of Halifax County in 1760 and held the post as a sinecure until 1773. Hitherto, however, identification of the clerk of Halifax County has been uncertain because of the possibility that he was the dramatist's cousin Robert Munford of Amelia. Since the Clerk of Halifax was never sued there, it can be assumed that he was not a third Robert Munford, of Halifax.

Ascertaining the identity of the Clerk by means of signatures is unfortunately not a simple matter. No sample of the script of RM of Amelia is known to this writer; and only three letters from RM of Mecklenburg are extant from the period, dated 1756, 1757, and 1775. The signatures and script of these three letters are all quite different. To check these against the script of the Clerk is not easy, even though the loose papers of the court are still available, because deputies William Wright and Thomas Tunstall obviously signed for the Clerk.

Since the Clerk was supposed to attend the monthly meetings of the county court, the presence of one RM elsewhere on these dates would theoretically eliminate him. Unfortunately this test eliminates both: the Clerk allegedly signed on 19 March 1767 while RM of Amelia was attending the House of Burgesses and on 16 November 1769 and 21 June 1770 while RM of Mecklenburg was attending. Thus Tunstall must have at least occasionally signed for the Clerk. The practice was probably routine.

Denied an easy and sure method of identification, one is forced to rely instead upon probability. The evidence, all of it pointing to RM of Mecklenburg, can be arranged as that from a priori suitability, association, and chronology. A priori, George Currie would more likely defer to his stepson than to his wife's deceased husband's nephew; and at Williamsburg Governor Nelson was likely to be willing to name as clerk a man trained in law under Peyton Randolph. Concerning RM of Amelia there seems to be no record of legal training or experience except that of magistrate. Moreover, in Halifax County the County Lieutenant was Richard Bland, uncle of RM of Mecklenburg; and the largest landowner was his friend and commanding officer William Byrd III, who in 1775 held 40,000 acres there and, as a member of the Council, had the ear of the governor.

The most numerous bits of evidence involve ties or associations, and many of these also involve chronology. First, there are no definitely established ties between RM of Amelia and Halifax County. But RM of Mecklenburg practiced law in Halifax, beginning his practice there the very next session after the Clerk was replaced. Moreover, in 1773, RM of Mecklenburg was briefly a vestryman of Antrim Parish, according to Mrs. Wirt Johnson Carrington's "Extracts from the First Vestry Book of Antrim Parish," in *W. & M.*, 2 Ser., VII (1927), 63. Secondly, although there seem to have been no Halifax-Amelia lawsuits involving RM of Amelia, several such suits show RM of Mecklenburg involved in Halifax. Thomas Cobbs, former Halifax County sheriff who had been sued by the Clerk on 20 October 1763 for his 1762 fees, sued RM of Mecklenburg in a long litigation delayed from 1767 to 1779; one of his witnesses was Colonel Wooding of Halifax, before whom the Clerk had permitted payment of fees to be established in the Halifax suit. In a suit brought by Joseph Abbott of Halifax County against RM of Mecklenburg, one of the witnesses was Thomas Wright, the Clerk's first deputy.

The evidence of chronology makes the identification well-nigh certain. In 1760 and 1761 RM of Mecklenburg received licenses to practice law in Lunenburg and evidently in Amelia. Then for twelve years, while a RM was

Clerk of Halifax, RM of Mecklenburg ceased to practice law. Then in September, 1772, when the Clerk was expecting dismissal, RM of Mecklenburg was again licensed to practice in Mecklenburg, and on 18 February 1773, just after the dismissal of the Clerk, RM of Mecklenburg was licensed to practice law in Halifax. One is tempted to infer that the impending loss of the Clerkship is referred to in a letter which Matthew Phipps wrote on 16 May 1772 to Theoderick Munford: "Your Brother tells me the great disappointment He's met with puts it out of his power to settle his account which I fancy has given him no small uneasiness" (Virginia Historical Society). This series of coincidents does not absolutely prove that the Clerk was RM of Mecklenburg, but the coefficient of probability is so high that without some evidence to the contrary—and none has appeared—it must be assumed that the Clerk of Halifax County was Robert Munford of Mecklenburg.

56. Clement, p. 72, citing Dinwiddie Papers, 11688.
57. Halifax Pleas, IV, 1.
58. The balance of Munford's 1762 fees, on 20 October 1763, was £338/3/4½ (Halifax Pleas, IV, 222).
59. Lunenburg Order Book, VI, 147 verso; Amelia County Pleas, VI, 227.
60. Lunenburg County Deed Book, X, 35-37, registered 13 December 1764.
61. Lunenburg Order Book, VII, 71 verso; MOB, IV, 390.
62. Lunenburg Order Book, VII, 71 verso.
63. Purdie and Dixon *Va. Gaz.*, 2 May 1776, p. 3.
64. Lunenburg Order Book, IX, 296.
65. "Justices of the Peace of Colonial Virginia," ed. H. R. McIlwaine, in Virginia State Library *Bulletin*, XIV (1921), 65; MOB, I, 3.
66. Hening, VIII, 141.
67. MOB, I, 175.

CHAPTER III

1. Andrew Burnaby, *Travels through North America*, ed. Rufus Wilson (New York, 1904), pp. 33-35.
2. Lyon Gardiner Tyler, *Williamsburg, the Old Colonial Capitol* (Richmond, 1907), p. 107.
3. "Journal of a French Traveller in the Colonies, 1765," in *American Historical Review*, XXVI (1920-1921), 741-742. Evidently some of Sir Peyton's friends called him "Skipper," as St. George Tucker addressed his "dearest Aunt Skipper," in a poem of 15 April 1815 (Prince, p. 238, quoting Tucker-Coleman MSS).
4. Robert Douthat Meade, *Patrick Henry, Patriot in the Making* (Philadelphia, 1957), p. 169, quoting the 1815 Memo by Paul Carrington in the Library of Congress.
5. Dumas Malone, *Jefferson the Virginian* (Boston, 1948), p. 93.
6. Paul Carrington to William Wirt, in William Wirt Henry, *Patrick Henry* (New York, 1891), I, 86 and 82n.
7. David John Mays, *Edmund Pendleton, 1721-1803* (Cambridge, Mass., 1952), I, 163, quoting Fauquier to the Lords of Trade, 5 June 1765.
8. *JHB, 1766-1769*, p. 53.
9. *Ibid.*, pp. 11, 15, 43.
10. Mays, I, 181. Munford evidently attended court in Mecklenburg County on 9 March, and his name is missing from the scanty records of the House for this session. Nevertheless he probably attended, arriving late.
11. MOB, I, 425-427; II, 23; II, 55.
12. MOB, II, 115; II, 178; II, 218.
13. Rind *Va. Gaz.*, 28 April 1768, p. 3.
14. He arrived late at the Mecklenburg Court on 14 March (MOB, I, 477) and was late also on 11 April (MOB, I, 488).

15. *JHB, 1766-1769,* pp. 190-191.

16. *Ibid.,* pp. 214, 215.

17. *Ibid.,* p. xlii.

18. Princess Anne County, *Marriages of Princess Anne County, Virginia,* compiled and published by Elizabeth B. Wingo (n. p., 1961), pp. 74, 51.

19. *JHB, 1766-1769,* p. 294.

20. *Ibid.,* p. 352.

21. Elizabeth Beverley Kennon to Rachel Mordecai, 6 December 1813, in "Kennon Letters," *Va. Mag.,* XXXV (1927), 289; there are numerous notices in the *Va. Gaz.* The date of Anna Munford Currie's death is fixed in a letter from her brother Col. Theoderick Bland to John Randolph of Bizarre, 18 February 1771: "My sister Curry died two weeks ago" (Virginia Historical Society).

22. *JHB, 1770-1772,* p. 239.

23. Virginia, House of Burgesses, Miscellaneous Papers, Petition of Thomas Tunstall. The petition is printed in *JHB, 1773-1776,* p. 115, and in Mrs. Wirt Johnson Carrington, *A History of Halifax County* (Richmond, 1924), pp. 341-342. Tunstall was sued by Sheriff Wooding, in April, 1772, for £39/18/1½ (Halifax Pleas, VII, 310). Tunstall's reference in 1774 to "Robert Munford, Esq." would surely indicate Robert Munford of Mecklenburg, the only Munford who was then a burgess.

24. Halifax Pleas, VIII, 4. He had already acted as clerk on 3 January 1773 (Halifax Pleas, VII, 548-599).

25. *JHB, 1770-1772,* p. 159.

26. Virginia Historical Society.

27. MOB, III, 321; Halifax Pleas, VIII, 9.

28. *JHB, 1770-1772,* p. 212.

29. Purdie and Dixon *Va. Gaz.,* 8 October 1772, p. 3.

30. *Bland Papers,* I, 50; MOB, IV, 191.

31. George F. Norton to John Hatley Norton, of York Town, dated London, 14 July 1773, in *John Norton and Sons, Merchants of London and Virginia,* ed. Frances Norton Mason (Richmond, 1937), p. 337; Mecklenburg Deed Book, III, 171.

32. *JHB, 1773-1776,* p. 102.

33. *Ibid.,* p. xiv.

34. "An Interesting Colonial Document," *Va. Mag.,* XXVIII (1920), 56-57.

35. He had just served as chairman for the meeting of the Mecklenburg freeholders, and the Purdie and Dixon *Va. Gaz.* for 25 August 1774 (p. 2) announced him just elected. He was not present at the Mecklenburg Court of 8 August 1774.

36. H. J. Eckenrode, *The Revolution in Virginia* (Boston, 1916), pp. 34-35).

37. From the original in the Virginia Historical Society.

38. Dixon and Hunter *Va. Gaz.,* 3 June 1775, p. 3.

39. MOB, IV, 304.

40. Dixon and Hunter *Va. Gaz.,* 3 June 1775, p. 3.

41. Malone, p. 198.

42. *Ibid.,* pp. 198-199; *JHB, 1773-1776,* pp. 177, 187-188.

43. *Ibid.,* pp. 189, 193-194, 194-195, 223-224, 249.

44. *Ibid.,* pp. 207-208.

CHAPTER IV

1. Hening, IX, 9.

2. *Ibid.,* IX, 20-21.

3. *Ibid.,* IX, 29.

4. *Ibid.,* IX, 27.

5. Dixon and Hunter *Va. Gaz.,* 21 October 1775, p. 2.

6. Virginia, *Calendar of Virginia State Papers,* ed. H. W. Flournoy, William

P. Palmer, *et al.* (Richmond, 1875-1893), VIII, 97. Subsequent references will cite merely *CSP.* Herbert A. Elliott, letter to William B. Hill, 30 April 1964.

7. Hening, IX, 78.

8. Virginia, Council, *Journals of the Council of the State of Virginia.* ed. H. R. McIlwaine (Richmond, 1931-1932), II, 452. Munford actually received the money twice.

9. *CSP,* VIII, 87-88.

10. *CSP,* VIII, 203; Elliott to Hill, as above; *Revolutionary War Records, Mecklenburg County,* pp. 14, 53.

11. Hening, IX, 116-117.

12. "Virginia Militia in the Revolution," in *Va. Mag.,* VI (1898-1899), 219, 401-403; VIII (1900-1901), 308.

13. Hening, IX, 140.

14. MOB, IV, 362, 366.

15. *JHD, May, 1779,* p. 6; Malone, p. 258; Hening, X, 50-65.

16. *JHD, May, 1779,* p. 28.

17. *Ibid.,* p. 39.

18. *JHD, October, 1779,* p. 55.

19. *Ibid.,* pp. 56, 83-84; George E. Lewis, *The Indiana Company, 1763-1798* (Glendale, Cal., 1941), p. 233.

20. *JHD, May, 1779,* p. 6.

21. *Ibid.,* p. 32

22. Kate Mason Rowland, *The Life of George Mason* (New York, 1892), I, 335.

23. *JHD, May, 1779,* p. 45; Malone, pp. 318-319.

24. *JHD, May, 1779,* p. 7.

25. *Ibid., p.* 32.

26. *Virginia Militia in the Revolutionary War,* ed. J. T. McAllister, (Hot Springs, Va. 1913), pp. 142-143, 144-145; Henry Lee, *Memoirs of the War in the Southern Department,* new ed. by Robert E. Lee (New York, 1870), pp. 129-130; Edward McCrady, *The History of South Carolina in the Revolution, 1775-1780* (New York, 1902), pp. 387-389. According to a letter from Mr. Herbert Elliott to Mr. William B. Hill, 30 April 1964, "The muster roll of Captain Reuben Vaughan's Company (1779), now in the University of North Carolina Library . . . , lists this company as under the command of Colonel David Mason. . . ." See also *Revolutionary War Records, Mecklenburg County,* p. 162.

27. Lee, p. 131.

28. *JHD, October, 1779,* pp. 6, 7.

29. *Ibid.,* p. 52.

30. *Ibid.,* p. 10.

31. *Ibid.,* p. 13.

32. *Ibid.,* p.15.

33. *Ibid.,* pp. 15, 80; Hening, X, 205-207.

34. *JHD, October, 1779,* p. 13.

35. *Ibid.,* p. 18.

36. *Ibid.,* pp. 12, 22, 35.

37. *Ibid.,* p. 25.

38. *Ibid.,* p. 27.

39. *Ibid.,* pp. 48, 49.

40. *Ibid.,* pp. 25, 29.

41. *JHD, May, 1779,* p. 32.

42. *JHD, October, 1779,* p. 33.

43. *Ibid.,* p. 15.

44. *Ibid.,* pp. 13-14, 26, 87.

45. *Ibid.,* pp. 16, 79.

46. *Ibid.*, p. 42.

47. *Ibid.*, pp. 44, 54.

48. *Ibid.*, pp. 26, 36.

49. *Ibid.*, p. 74.

50. *Ibid.*, pp. 76-77, 99.

51. Hening, X, 215.

52. Eckenrode, p. 203.

53. Mrs. Elizabeth H. Farley to Mrs. Frances Randolph, 6 July 1778, Library of Colonial Williamsburg.

54. Mecklenburg County, *The Marriage License Bonds of Mecklenburg County, Virginia from 1765 to 1810*, abstracted by John Y. Hutcheson and listed by Stratton Nottingham (Onancock, Va., 1928), p. 30.

55. "Kennon Letters," in *Va. Mag.*, XXXI, (1923), 186; "Kennon Family," in *W. & M.*, 1 Ser., XIV (1905-1906), 135.

56. MOB, V, 34; St. George Tucker, "Robin Hood, a Tale," in William Munford's Miscellany, pp. 88-89, in the Duke University Library. The poem incorrectly dates the marriage in May, 1781; Tucker was in command of his militia at that time, and Anne Beverley Kennon was born 4 May 1781 (McGill, p. 616).

57. *JHD, May, 1780*, p. 40.

58. Thomas Person to Governor Thomas Burke, 26 July 1781, in North Carolina, *State Records*, XV, 575-576.

59. Munford to General Nathanael Greene, Richland, 31 December 1781, from a microfilm copy of the original in the Clements Library, the University of Michigan. Some conventional contractions have been expanded "Mr. Colcock" was probably John Colcock, attorney, recently Secretary to the Privy Council of South Carolina. See A. S. Salley, Jr., "Capt. John Colcock and Some of his Descendants." *South Carolina Historical and Genealogical Magazine*, III (1902), 219-220.

60. Munford to Greene, Richland, 13 July 1781, *loc cit.*

61. Stevens to Jefferson, 20 August 1780, in Jefferson, *Papers*, ed. Julian P. Boyd *et al* (Princeton, 1951–), III, 558-559.

62. North Carolina, *State Records*, XIV, 576, corrected by the writer from a positive in the Library of Congress of the original in the New York Historical Society.

63. *Ibid.*, XIV, 614, corrected as above.

64. Hening, X, 263-267.

65. From a microfilm in the Library of Congress of the Gates Papers, New York Historical Society.

66. Jefferson, *Papers*, III, 576-577.

67. Munford to General Gates, 28 August 1780, in North Carolina, *State Records*, XIV, 577.

68. Gist to Munford, Baltimore, 24 October 1780, from a photostat of the Gist letterbook in the Maryland Historical Society. The letter was printed in *Maryland Historical Magazine*, IV (1909), 369-372.

69. *JHD, October, 1780*, pp. 14, 36.

70. *Ibid.*, p. 67.

71. From a microfilm in the Library of Congress of the Gates Papers in the New York Historical Society; Jefferson, *Papers*, IV, 461.

72. Munford wrote two letters to General Greene, on 24 February and 1 March 1781, from Taylor's Ferry; and a receipt signed "Robert Munford, QM," (George Rogers Clark MSS, Virginia State Library, photocopy in serial C, I, 274) evidently places him there on 10 March 1781 acting as Quartermaster, for the Colonel (Raleigh P.) Downman mentioned in the receipt was on this very day having trouble with the Amelia militia on the way to Guildford Court House (*CSP, I, 559*). Citing the above receipt, John H. Gwathmey, in his

Historical Register of Virginians in the Revolution (Richmond, 1938), p. 572, seems to have created a ghost Robert Munford "Q. M. at Fort Jefferson in 1781." Although Virginia maps from midcentury show a Jefferson in Mecklenburg County on the Roanoke River, it is not designated "Fort Jefferson," and it is shown as several miles downstream from Taylor's Ferry. According to Mr. Herbert Elliott (*loc. cit.*), Captains James Anderson and Benjamin Ferrell also acted as quartermaster here.

73. For details of supplies, see "Revolutionary Pension Declarations," in *Va. Mag.*, XX (1912), 261; Virginia, Public Service Claims, Mecklenburg County, Court Booklet, pp. 4, 7, 14, 15; Public Service Claims, Mecklenburg County, Lists, pp. 9, 10; Public Service Claims, Mecklenburg County, Commissioners Book, IV, 67, 349. Wheelright Billy is mentioned in the 1789 Inventory, Mecklenburg Will Book, III, 19.

74. Jefferson, *Papers*, IV, 208.

75. North Carolina, *State Records*, XIV, 762.

76. According to the 1840 deposition of Clement Blackbourn (Dorman, VII, 29-30), who was ordered out in August, 1780 for three months' guard duty at the magazine, it was removed after about two months. But see Lucy Kate McGhee, *Virginia Pension Abstracts* (Washington, 1959–) XII, 98; V, 98. Carrington is named commanding "General" for the summer of 1781 by John Allgood in his 1833 deposition (Dorman, I, 87).

77. Jefferson, *Papers*, IV, 294-295, 352.

78. On 12 February 1781, among militia recommended by the Mecklenburg Court "to fill up the vacancies," was Lewis Burwell as county lieutenant (MOB, V, 91).

79. Greene to Munford, Pendleton's copy, in the Clements Library, University of Michigan.

80. *CSP*, I, 540.

81. Burwell to Greene, 5 March 1781, in the Clements Library, the University of Michigan.

82. *Loc. cit.*

83. Pendleton to Munford, Pendleton's copy, *loc. cit.* The original copy, verbatim as cited, is quoted in part in Jay B. Hubbell, *The South in American Literature* (Durham, N. C. 1954), p. 144n. 13.

84. Tucker-Coleman Collection in Colonial Williamsburg. Tucker unintentionally gave "3000" as the number "with us."

85. Clements Library, University of Michigan.

86. *Loc. cit.*

87. Tucker-Coleman Papers, Colonial Williamsburg. This letter was published by Charles W. Coleman, Jr., "The Southern Campaign," in *Magazine of American History*, VII (1881), 40-42; and in Mary Haldane Coleman, *St. George Tucker, Citizen of No Mean City* (Richmond, 1938), pp. 55-58. The Beverley mentioned in the account was Col. Beverley Randolph.

88. Clements Library, University of Michigan.

89. *Loc. cit.*

90. *Loc. cit.*

91. *Loc. cit.*

92. Burwell to Archibald Blair, 9 September 1781, *CSP*, II, 407; to Governor Nelson, dated Newsum's Old Field, 26 September 1781, *CSP*, II, 492; to Nelson, 30 September 1781, *CSP*, II, 510.

93. They were married before 18 October 1781 (Mecklenburg Deed Book, VI, 142).

94. "Letters of the Byrd Family," *Va. Mag.*, XXXIX (1931), 223-224, 226, 227; "Will of Colonel William Byrd, 3d.," in *ibid.*, IX (1901-1902), 81, 86-87; John Richard Alden, *General Charles Lee, Traitor or Patriot?* (Baton Rouge, 1951), pp. 51, 627; "Major General Charles Lee's Will," *Va. Mag.*, XI (1903-1904), 109.

95. Mrs. Farley to Capt. Thomas Taylor Byrd, 25 June 1783.

96. Indenture of bargain and sale was recorded in MOB, V, 159, and V, 262.

97. "The Fitzhugh Family," *Va. Mag.*, VIII (1900-1901), 93.

98. Jackson T. Main, "The One Hundred," *W. & M.*, 3 Ser., XI (1954), 375.

99. *CSP*, III, 162.

100. MOB, V, 142, 193.

101. MOB, V, 278.

102. MOB, V, 286.

103. MOB, V, 315, 320, 358, 359, 482, 502.

104. Letter Book, Library of Congress, from microfilm in the Virginia State Library.

105. *Kennon vs. McRobert*, in Virginia, Supreme Court of Appeals, *Reports*, I, 97; and *Seekright vs. Hood*, Prince Edward County District Court, Order Book, 1789-1792, p. 32.

106. Mecklenburg Will Book, II, 45.

107. "Diary of Richard N. Venable, 1791-92," *Tyler's Quarterly Historical and Genealogical Magazine*, II (Oct., 1920), 138.

108. William Munford, Account Book, p. 128, from Duke University microfilm of original in the Huntington Library; Sarah Short Skipwith Kennon to Rachel Mordecai, 9 July 1809, in "Some Kennon Letters," *Va. Mag.*, XXXI (1923), 312.

109. Anna (Munford) Byrd to George Wythe Munford, Lynchburg, 23 May 1836. Munford-Ellis Papers, Duke University Library. The quotation comes from William Munford's(?) Prologue to *The Candidates*.

CHAPTER V

1. William Byrd II, Book Sale Catalogue, in Byrd, *Writings*, ed. Bassett (New York, 1901), pp. 413-443.

2. See Robert N. Land, "The Theatre in Colonial Virginia," Master's thesis, University of Virginia, 1936; and Hugh F. Rankin, *The Theater in Colonial America* (Chapel Hill, 1960, 1965).

3. William Munford to John Coalter, 10 November 1792, in "Glimpses of Old College Life," *W. & M.*, 1 Ser., VIII (1899-1900), 156.

4. Both of Munford's plays were first published in *A Collection of Plays and Poems by the late Colonel Robert Munford, of Mecklenburg, in the State of Virginia* (Petersburg, 1798). All references cite the Readex microprint of the copy of the American Antiquarian Society. As Mr. Edwin Wolf, II, Librarian, Library Company of Philadelphia, points out in a letter, 4 February 1964, to the writer, there are some variations in sheet C, pp. 17-24, in the early scenes of *The Candidates*.

5. Courtlandt Canby, Preface to Munford, *The Patriots*, *W. & M.*, 3 Ser., VI (1949), 446 n. 21.

6. Lunenburg Order Book, VII, 23 verso.

7. Mecklenburg Deed Book, II, 256-257.

8. On 10 April 1782 Munford presented public service claims for, *inter alia*, £99 "for the use of 2 Sceins & 2 fishing places on Roan Oak river during the season of Catching Shads." Virginia, Public Service Claims, Mecklenburg County, Court Booklet, p. 14. See also Commissioners Book, IV, 349.

9. Rind *Va. Mag.*, 15 July 1773, p. 4; Purdie *Va. Gaz.*, 9 May 1777, p. 3; Charlotte Orders, I, 6 verso.

10. MOB, III, 166.

11. MOB, IV, 436; IV, 447.

12. Dixon and Nicholson Virginia *Gazette*, 21 August 1779, p. 4. In his edition of his father's plays and poems, the identifying initials and county are omitted.

13. Elizabeth Beverley Kennon to Samuel Mordecai, Mecklenburg, 24 December 1815, in "Some Kennon Letters," *Va. Mag.*, XXXVIII (1930), 366.

14. MOB, III, 27, 52.

15. Edgar, pp. 39-40, 98, 269, 381, 402, 469, 487, 508, 536.

16. Rose Chambers Goode McCullough, *Yesterday When it is Past* (Richmond, 1957), p. 54.

17. Edgar, p. 249.

18. Dixon and Hunter *Va. Gaz.*, 18 March 1775.

19. Fairfax Harrison, *The Roanoke Stud, 1795-1833* (Richmond, 1930), pp. 71-73, citing *American Turf Register*, ed. J. S. Skinner, III, 450; Edgar, pp. 537-538; Nat Hutcheson, p. 17; W. A. De Laney, "Debunks Legend of Polly Williams' Untimely Demise," Richmond *News Leader*, 28 November 1961. Mr. De Laney kindly sent the writer an exhaustive bibliography of the Polly Williams legend and generously answered in detail a number of queries.

20. Speed, p. 166.

21. MOB, II, 501, 518; III, 40, 67.

22. Dixon and Hunter *Va. Gaz.*, 3 June 1775, p. 3.

23. Speed, pp. 27, 59, 62, 58; William Wirt Henry, "House of Burgesses, 1766 to 1775," *Va. Mag.*, IV (1896-1897), 384.

24. MOB, II, 273, 484.

25. *Flagel* (London, 1768), pp. 80, 71, 10, 42.

26. Henry Fielding, *The Complete Works of Henry Fielding*, ed. William Henley (London, 1903), XI, 30.

27. Miles Peter Andrews, *The Election* (London, 1774), p. 6.

28. *JHB, 1736-1740*, pp. 246, 282.

29. *JHB, 1761-1765*, pp. 358-359.

30. *JHB, 1766-1769*, pp. 17, 54.

31. *Ibid.*, p. 206.

32. *JHB, 1770-1772*, pp. 21-29.

33. *Bland Papers*, I, 27.

34. George Washington, *The Writings of George Washington*, ed. John C. Fitzpatrick (Washington, 1931-1944), II, 241-242n.

35. *JHB, 1752-1755, 1756-1758*, pp. 339, 421, 456-457.

36. *Ibid.*, p. 83.

37. *JHB, 1766-1769*, p. 231.

38. *Ibid.*, p. 243.

39. *JHB, 1752-1755, 1756-1758*, p. 84.

40. Samuel Foote, *The Mayor of Garratt*, ed. Dibden (London, 1815), p. 20.

41. *JHB, 1766-1769*, pp. 54, 130; Hening, VIII, 257.

42. *JHB, 1766-1769*, pp. 269, 320; Hening, VIII, 392.

43. *JHB, 1758-1761.* p. 212.

44. *JHB, 1766-1769*, p. 86.

CHAPTER VI

1. Arthur Hobson Quinn, *A History of the American Drama from the Beginning to the Civil War*, 2nd. ed. (New York, 1951), pp. 54, 473.

2. William Dunlap, *A History of the American Theatre* (New York, 1963), p. 64. Quinn, p. 32, cites the resolution of 20 October 1774 as printed in the *Journals of the Continental Congress, 1774-1789*, ed. Ford (Washington, 1904), I, 78.

3. William Munford, *Poems and Compositions in Prose* (Richmond, 1798), p. 148n. Mr. William B. Hill to the writer, 4 May 1964 .

4. McCullough, p. 57.

5. Dixon and Hunter *Va. Gaz.*, 3 June 1775, p. 3.

6. McCullough, p. 57. By 13 October 1777 he was a full Colonel (MOB, IV, 374).

7. Virginia, House of Delegates, Mecklenburg Petition 392, Virginia State Library.

8. McCullough, p. 57.

9. North Carolina *State Records*, XVIII, 449, 458.

10. G. Brown Goode, *Virginia Cousins* (Richmond, 1887), p. 67.

11. G. O. Selihamer, *History of the American Theatre* (Philadelphia, 1888-1891), I, 282.

12. David Garrick, *Miss in her Teens* (London, 1747), p. 13.

13. Flash maintains, "I'm not to be frighten'd with Squibs, Madam, no, no" (*Ibid.*, p. 26).

14. *Ibid.*, pp. 25-26. Among other borrowings from Farquhar's *Recruiting Officer*, part of the dialogue between Melinda and Silva (Act I, scene iii) seems in part adapted by Munford in Act II, scene iii (p. 83).

15. George Farquhar, *The Complete Works of George Farquhar*, ed. Charles Stonehill (London, 1930), II, 50.

16. Colley Cibber, *Damon and Phillida* (London, 1729), p. 20.

17. Henry Carey, *The Honest Yorkshire-Man* (London, 1736), p. 8.

18. Joseph Wood Krutch, *Comedy and Conscience After the Restoration* (New York, 1961), p. 213.

19. CSP, VIII, 97; Virginia, Council of State, *Journals of the Council of the State of Virginia*, II, 171; MOB, V, 298-299.

20. Eckenrode, p. 206.

21. Dixon and Hunter *Va. Gaz.*, 3 June 1775, p. 3.

22. See Cumberland County Committee of Correspondence, *Proceedings of the Committees of Safety of Cumberland and Isle of Wight Counties, Virginia.* ed. H. R. McIlwaine, in Virginia, State Library, *Fifteenth Annual Report* (Richmond, 1919).

23. MOB, IV, 371, 374.

24. His descendant Mr. Wesley Alleyn De Laney reports, in a letter of 23 July 1963, a family tradition concerning Deloney's war record: "Family tradition which in nearly every instance has been substantiated fully, has it that Deloney left Mecklenburg in 1778 to try to get a cavalry command under Washington whom he knew as a burgess. Somewhere on his long ride north he became involved in a skirmish with the enemy and lost a leg as a result of a fall from his horse. In Pennsylvania or New Jersey or elsewhere we do not know. We assumed that he never had the chance to get the commission he sought. . . . The tradition is that he returned to Virginia several months later and this was his first and last combat in the war." If this tradition is accurate, then either Deloney did not sit for Colonel Simple, or Munford surely wrote the play before Deloney came home a cripple. But Virginia Public Claims, Mecklenburg County, Certificates (Virginia State Library) show Deloney acting as Commissioner of Provisions from 5 September to 8 November 1781. Subsequently he was tried by jury on 10 September 1782 (MOB, V, 228) and assessed £33/6/8 for refusing to serve as a Commissioner of the Tax. Deloney's continued activity would seem to belie the family tradition; at any rate it remains unsubstantiated. According to the 1833 and 1834 testimony of Joseph Bennett of Mecklenburg County, he volunteered in the spring of 1776 in the regiment of Colonel Delaney, who "returned home." (Dorman, VI, 46, 47) Evidently Deloney officially embodied a unit of minute men who marched on 1 April 1776 from his own ordinary, but no evidence has come to light to show Deloney in combat.

Concerning Munford's dislike of Deloney there exists a curious action in Mecklenburg Court 11 February 1782. Deloney had just secured the permission of the court to turn a road to run on his land (MOB, V, 114) when Munford arrived late. Munford insisted that a stipulation be added that "the New Road must be as plain as the old Road; or as even" (MOB, V, 119). In the margin the Clerk of the Court commented, "This Order was entered on the Minute Book by Robert Munford Gent rearly [sic] as it stands here."

25. MOB, IV, 334.

26. MOB, I, 457.

27. MOB, I, 48; Speed, p. 166.

28. Eckenrode, p. 155.

29. *Ibid.*, p. 110.

30. *Ibid.*, p. 117.

31. *Ibid.*, p. 118.

32. *Ibid.*, pp. 179-180.

33. MOB, IV, 364.

34. Eckenrode, p. 182; MOB, IV, 362.

35. "Jameson—Ellegood—Parker," *W. & M.*, 1 Ser., XIII (1904-1905), 69.

36. MOB, IV, 353.

37. MOB, IV, 371.

38. Speed, p. 167; *JHD, October 1779*, p. 56.

39. Virginia, House of Delegates, Petitions, 1775-1778, Mecklenburg, Petition 392. Virginia State Library.

40. Pinckney *Va. Gaz.*, 30 December 1775, p. 2.

41. Purdie *Va. Gaz.*, 20 December 1776, Supplement, p. 2.

42. *Burke's Genealogical and Heraldic History of the Peerage, Baronetage and Knightage*, 99th ed. (London, 1949), p. 1850.

43. Sir Peyton produced a commission as sheriff 10 March 1777 (MOB, IV, 346).

44. MOB, IV, 419.

45. MOB, V, 97.

46. Lorenzo Sabine, *Biographical Sketches of Loyalists of the American Revolution* (Boston, 1864), II, 309.

47. MOB, IV, 428, 466.

48. MOB, V, 82.

49. Spenser Roane to Governor Edmund Randolph, 3 September 1787, in *CSP*, IV, 338-339.

50. Beverley to Edmund Athawes, ante 6 July 1775. Beverley Letterbook in Library of Congress, from a microfilm in the Virginia State Library.

51. *Loc. cit.* This letter has been printed by Robert M. Calhoon in " 'A Sorrowful Spectator of these Tumultous Times': Robert Beverley Describes the Coming of the Revolution," in *Va. Mag.*, LXXIII (Jan., 1965), 41-55.

EPILOGUE: REDISCOVERY

1. The Library of the College of William and Mary.

2. Edward A. Wyatt IV, editor, *Preliminary Checklist for Petersburg, Virginia Imprint Series* Number 9 (Richmond, 1949), passim.

3. *Ibid.*, p. 16.

4. Mr. Edwin Wolfe II, Librarian, The Library Company of Philadelphia, to the writer, 4 February 1964. The assumption is the present writer's.

5. *Idem* and Library Company of Philadelphia, *A Catalogue of the Books Belonging to the Library Company* (Philadelphia, 1835), passim.

6. Mr. Edwin Wolfe II, as above.

7. Although the copyright was registered to Sarah Munford only, Nathaniel Beverley Tucker, their cousin, mentioned in his review that "Of all he left behind him, his sons, proud of a father who might well be proud of them, have selected a translation of Homer, which they offer to the world, as an evidence of his poetic talent, and classical attainments" (*Southern Literary Messenger*, XII [1846], 448).

8. *Southern Literary Messenger*, XII (1846), 446. The identification of the reviewers is made by Mr. Jay B. Hubbell, in his *The South in American Literature*, p. 951.

9. This copy is owned by Mrs. Mary Haldane Coleman, of Williamsburg.

10. *The North American Review*, LXIII (July, 1846), 151.

11. *The Southern Quarterly Review*, X (1846), p. 2 and n.

12. Rufus Wilmot Griswold, *Poets and Poetry of America*, 10th ed. (Philadelphia, 1850), p. 68.

13. Evert A. and George L. Duyckinck, eds., *Cyclopaedia of American Literature* (New York, 1856), I, 642.

14. Mr. Edwin Wolfe II, as above.

15. Mr. Frederick R. Goff, Chief, Rare Book Division, to the writer, 13 February 1964. "The second copy is missing from the shelves," Mr. Goff writes, "and cannot be located."

16. Mr. John Alden, Keeper of Rare Books, Boston Public Library, to the writer, 13 February 1964.

17. Joseph Sabin, *Bibliotheca Americana* (New York, 1868-1936), I, xi (Prospectus).

18. *Ibid.*, XIV, 239. The brackets are in the original.

19. Mr. Roger E. Stoddard, Curator, Harriss Collection of American Poetry and Plays, Brown University Library, to the writer, 7 February 1964.

20. George O. Seilhamer, *History of the American Theatre* (Philadelphia, 1888-1891), II, 13-15.

21. Oscar Wegelin, *Early American Plays, 1714-1830* (New York, 1900), pp. 5, 72, 112; 2nd ed. (New York, 1905), pp. 16, 58, 93. In his *Early American Poetry*, 2nd ed. (New York, 1930) Wegelin transcribed (p. 57) the title page of the Brown University copy.

22. Louise Manly, *Southern Literature* (Richmond, 1895) p. 493; Sidney Ernest Bradshaw, *On Southern Poetry Prior to 1860* (Richmond, 1900), pp. 35-36.

23. Lyon G. Tyler, "Education in Colonial Virginia, Part IV, The Higher Education," *W. & M.*, 1 Ser., VI (1897-1898), 175.

24. Mr. Milton C. Russell, Head, Reference and Circulation Section, Virginia State Library, to the writer, 6 February 1964; interview with Mrs. Coleman, July, 1963; Miss Josephine Nunnally, Acting Librarian, University of Richmond Library, to the writer, 4 February 1964.

25. Additional copies are the J. B. Clopton-Charles M. Wallace copy acquired in 1909 by the John Carter Brown Library (Mr. Glenn B. Skillin to the author, 6 February 1964) and the Albert Gorton Greene-Harriss-Henry B. Anthony copy acquired by the University of Chicago "about fifty years ago" (Mr. Robert Rosenthal, Curator, Special Collections, to the writer, 4 February 1964).

26. Montrose J. Moses, *Literature of the South* (New York, 1910), p. 158.

27 Montrose J. Moses, *The American Dramatist* (Boston, 1925), p. 52.

28. Arthur Hobson Quinn, *A History of the American Drama from the Beginning to the Civil War* (New York, 1923), pp. 54, 448; Library Company of Philadelphia, *Catalogue*, I, 516; Quinn, 2nd. ed. (New York, 1951), pp. 54, 473.

29. Mr. Barney Chesnick, Curator, Philadelphia Library Co., to the writer.

30. Mr. Frederick R. Goff, as above; that the Parsons copy is the 1798 edition is obvious in the *Early American Imprint* series, where it is reproduced in microprint. According to Mr. Marcus McCorison, Librarian of the American Antiquarian Society, the copy, secured in 1937, was probably owned by Alexander Parsons (letter to the writer, 3 February 1964).

31. William and Mary Library.

32. *The Literature of the South*, ed. Richmond Croom Beatty, Floyd C. Watkins, and Thomas Daniel Young (Chicago, 1952), p. 5.

Bibliography

List of Short Titles Most Frequently Cited in Footnotes

CSP — Virginia. *Calendar of Virginia State Papers*. Richmond, 1875-1893.

Hening — Virginia, General Assembly. *The Statutes at Large; Being a Collection of all the Laws of Virginia*, ed. William Walter Hening. Richmond, 1809-1823.

JHB — Virginia, House of Burgesses. *Journals of the House of Burgesses of Virginia*, ed. John P. Kennedy and H. R. McIlwaine. Richmond, 1905-1915.

JHD — Virginia, House of Delegates. *Journal of the House of Delegates of Virginia*. Richmond, 1827.

MOB — Mecklenburg County Order Books.

Va. Gaz. — *The Virginia Gazette*.

Va. Mag. — *The Virginia Magazine of History and Biography*.

W. & M. — *The William and Mary Quarterly*.

UNPUBLISHED MATERIAL

Amelia County Pleas. Like all other county papers except for some of those of Mecklenburg and Halifax counties, these were consulted in the microfilm copies at the Virginia State Library.

Berwick, Keith B. "Loyalties in Crisis: a Study of the Attitudes of Virginians in the Revolution." Unpublished doctoral dissertation, The University of Chicago, 1959.

Beverley, Elizabeth. Correspondence. Virginia Historical Society.

Beverley, Robert. Letter Book. Library of Congress (consulted in microfilm copy in the Virginia State Library).

——————. Papers. Virginia Historical Society.

Beverley, William. Papers, especially 1750 Memorandum Book. Virginia Historical Society.

——————. Letters. New York Public Library (microfilm copies in the Virginia State Library).

Brunswick County Order Books.

Burwell, Lewis. See Greene.

115

Byrd, Anna (Munford). Correspondence with George Wythe Munford. Munford-Ellis Papers. Duke University Library.

Charlotte County Orders.

Clarke, George Rogers. Manuscript Collection. Virginia State Library.

Farley, Mrs. Elizabeth H. (Byrd). Correspondence. Colonial Williamsburg.

Gist, Mordecai. Letter Book. Maryland Historical Society, consulted in a photostatic copy now in the Library of the University of Georgia.

Greene, Nathanael. Correspondence with Munford and Lewis Burwell. Clements Library, University of Michigan. Microfilm copies in the University of Georgia Library.

Halifax County Deeds.

Halifax County Loose Papers (Halifax County Court House).

Halifax County Pleas.

Henrico County Deeds. Wills, Etc., 1697-1704.

Henry County Order Books.

Kennon, Elizabeth Munford. Correspondence with Rachel and Samuel Mordecai. Typed copies of many letters still not printed in the *Virginia Magazine*. Virginia Historical Society and the E. A. Williams Family, of Baltimore.

Land, Robert Hunt. "Theatre in Colonial Virginia." Master's thesis at the University of Virginia, 1936. Microfilm copy in the University of Georgia Library.

Lunenburg County Deed Books.

Lunenburg County Order Books.

Mecklenburg County Deed Books.

Mecklenburg County Order Books. Cited as MOB.

Mecklenburg County Will Books.

Munford, Robert. Correspondence with Nathanael Greene. See Greene.

————————.Letter to William Byrd, III. Virginia Historical Society.

————————. Letters to General Horatio Gates. Gates Papers. New York Historical Society (positive copies in thhe Library of Congress), and Pennsylvania Historical Society.

————————. Letters to Theoderick Bland, Sr. Munford folder, Miscellaneous Papers, New York Public Library, and the Virginia Historical Society.

Munford, William. Account Book. Huntington Library. Consulted in the microfilm copy from the Duke University Library.

————————. Correspondence with John Coalter and Maria Rind. Library of the College of William and Mary.

————————. Miscellany, 1802-1814. Duke University Library.

Mutual Assurance Society of Virginia. Papers. Microfilm copy in the Virginia State Library.

Phipps, Matthew. Letter to Theoderick Munford. Bland-Campbell Papers. Virginia Historical Society.

Prince, William Stevens. "St. George Tucker as a Poet of the Early Republic." Yale doctoral dissertation, 1954.

Prince Edward County District Court Order Books.

Prince George County Minute Book, 1737-1740.

Prince George County Orders.

Tucker, St. George. Letters to Mrs. Tucker. Colonial Williamsburg.

―――――――. "Robin Hood, a Tale," copy in William Munford, Miscellany. Duke University Library.

Virginia Land Grants. Colonial Patents. Virginia State Library.

Virginia Public Service Claims. Certificates. Virginia State Library.

―――――――. Commissioners' Books. Virginia State Library.

―――――――. Court Booklets. Virginia State Library.

―――――――. Lists. Virginia State Library.

Virginia, House of Burgesses. Miscellaneous Papers. Virginia State Library.

Virginia, House of Delegates. Petitions, 1775-1778. Virginia State Library.

PUBLISHED MATERIAL

Alden, Edmund Kimball. "John Banister," *Dictionary of American Biography*, I, 576.

Alden, John Richard. *General Charles Lee: Traitor or Patriot?* Baton Rouge: Louisiana State University Press, 1951.

Andrews, Miles Peter. *New Musical Interlude Called the Election.* London, 1774.

Bell, Landon C. *Cumberland Parish, Lunenburg County, Virginia, 1746-1816: Vestry Book, 1746-1816.* Richmond: William Byrd Press, 1930.

Bland, Theoderick, Jr. *The Bland Papers.* Ed. Charles Campbell. 2 vols. Petersburg: E. and J. Ruffin, 1840-1843.

Bolling, Robert, of Chellowe. *A Memoir of a Portion of the Bolling Family in England and Virginia.* Trans. John Robertson, Jr., ed. T. H. Wynne, in *Wynne's Historical Documents from the Old Dominion.* Richmond: privately printed, 1868.

Borgman, Albert S. *The Life and Death of William Mountfort.* Cambridge: Harvard University Press, 1935.

Bouquet, Henry. *The Papers of Col. Henry Bouquet.* Ed. Sylvester K. Stevens, Donald H. Kent, *et al.* 2 vols. Harrisburg: Pennsylvania Historical Commission, 1940, 1951.

Bradshaw, Herbert Clarence. *History of Prince Edward County, Virginia.* Richmond: Dietz Press, 1955.

Bradshaw, Sidney Ernest. *On Southern Poetry Prior to 1860.* Richmond: B. F. Johnson, 1900.

Bristol Parish. *The Vestry Book and Register of Bristol Parish, Virginia, 1720-1789.* Ed. Churchill Gibson Chamberlayne. Richmond: privately printed, 1898.

Burke, Sir John Bernard. *Burke's Genealogical and Heraldic History of the Peerage, Baronetage and Knightage*. 99th ed. London: Burke's Peerage, 1949.

Burnaby, Andrew. *Travels through North America*. Ed. Rufus Wilson. New York: A. Wessels, 1904.

Byrd, William II, of Westover. *Another Secret Diary of William Byrd of Westover, 1739-1741*. Ed. Maude Woodfin and Marion Tinling. Richmond: Dietz Press, 1942.

——————————. *The Prose Works of William Byrd of Westover*: *Narratives of a Colonial Virginian*. Ed. Louis B. Wright. Cambridge: Harvard University Press, 1966.

——————————. *Secret Diary of William Byrd of Westover, 1709-1712*. Ed. Louis B. Wright and Marion Tinling. Richmond: Dietz Press, 1941.

——————————. *The Writings of "Colonel William Byrd, of Westover in Virginia, Esqre."* Ed. John Spenser Bassett. New York: Doubleday, Page, and Co., 1901.

Carey, Henry. *The Honest Yorkshire-Man*: *a Ballad Farce*. London: 1736.

Carrington, Mrs. Wirt Johnson. *A History of Halifax County*. Richmond: Appeals Press, 1924.

Charles City County. *Charles City County Court Orders*. Ed. Beverley Fleet. *Virginia Colonial Abstracts*, Vols. X, XIII. Baltimore: Genealogical Publishing Co., 1961.

Cibber, Colley. *Damon and Phillida*: *a Ballad Opera*. London, 1729.

Clement, Maud Carter. *The History of Pittsylvania County, Virginia*. Lynchburg: J. P. Bell Co., 1929.

Coleman, Charles W., Jr. "The Southern Campaign," *Magazine of American History*, VII (July, 1881), 36-46.

Coleman, Mary Haldane. *St. George Tucker, Citizen of No Mean City*. Richmond: Dietz Press, 1938.

Cumberland County Committee of Observation. *Proceedings of the Committees of Safety of Cumberland and Isle of Wight Counties, Virginia*. Ed. H. R. McIlwaine, in Virginia State Library. *Fifteenth Annual Report*. Richmond, 1919.

De Laney, W. A. "Debunks Legend of Polly Williams' Untimely Demise," Richmond *News Leader*, 28 November 1961.

Dorman, John Frederick, abstracter and compiler. *Virginia Revolutionary Pension Applications*. 6 vols. Washington: privately printed, 1958–.

Dunlap, William. *A History of the American Theatre*. 2d. ed. (3 vols. in one). New York: B. Franklin, 1963.

Duyckinck, Evert A. and George L., eds. *Cyclopaedia of American Literature*. 2 vols. New York: C. Scribner, 1856.

Eckenrode, H. J. *The Revolution in Virginia*. Boston: Houghton Mifflin, 1916.

Edgar, Patrick Nisbett. *The American Race-Turf Register, Sportsman's Herald, and General Stud Book.* New York: Henry Mason, 1833.

Eggleston, Joseph Dupuy. "Archibald McRobert, Patriot, Scholar, Man of God." Farmville, n.d. Reprinted from Farmville *Herald*, 20 April 1928.

The Election: a Comedy in Three Acts. London, 1749.

Farquhar, George. *The Complete Works of George Farquhar.* Ed. Charles Stonehill. 2 vols. London: Nonesuch Press, 1930.

Felton, Cornelius Conway. Review of William Munford's trans. of Homer's *Iliad. North American Review*, LXIII (July, 1846), 149-165.

Fielding, Henry. *Complete Works.* Ed. William Henley. 16 vols. London, 1903.

Flagel. London, 1768.

Foote, Samuel. *The Mayor of Garratt.* Vol. XVII of *The London Theatre.* Ed. Thomas Dibden. London, 1815.

Ford, Paul Leicester. *Washington and the Theatre.* New York: Dunlap Society, 1899.

Freeman, Douglas Southall, *Young Washington.* 2 vols. New York: C. Scribner's, 1948.

Garrick, David. *Miss in her Teens: or the Medley of Lovers.* London, 1747.

Georgia. *Colonial Records of the State of Georgia.* Ed. Allen D. Candler and Lucian Lamar Knight. 25 vols. Atlanta, 1904-1916.

Goode, G. Brown. *Virginia Cousins.* Richmond: J. W. Randolph and English, 1887.

Griswold, Rufus Wilmot. *The Poets and Poetry of America.* 10th ed., revised and enlarged. Philadelphia: Cary and Hart, 1850.

Gwathmey, John H. *Historical Register of Virginians in the Revolution.* Richmond: Dietz Press, 1938.

Harrell, Isaac Samuel. *Loyalism in Virginia.* Durham: Duke University Press, 1926.

Harrison, Fairfax. *The Roanoke Stud, 1795-1833.* Richmond: Old Dominion Press, 1930.

Hening, William. See Virginia, General Assembly. *Statutes at Large.*

Henry, William Wirt. *Patrick Henry: Life, Correspondence and Speeches.* 3 vols. New York: Scribner's, 1891.

Hervey, John. *Racing in America, 1665-1865.* 2 vols. New York: The Jockey Club, 1944.

Hill, William B., editor. *Land by the Roanoke: an Album of Mecklenburg County, Virginia.* Boydton, Va.: Roanoke River Branch, Association for the Protection of Virginia Antiquities, 1957.

Holmes, George F. Review of William Munford's translation of Homer's *Iliad, in Southern Quarterly Review*, X (July, 1846), 1-45.

Hubbell, Jay B. *The South in American Literature.* Durham: Duke University Press, 1954.

Hutcheson, Nat G. *What Do You Know about Horses? Mecklenburg County and the Aristocratic Thoroughbreds.* Boydton, Va.: privately printed, n.d.

Hutcheson, Sterling. "Richland Hill," Clarksville *Times* and Mecklenburg County *Record*, XII, No. 52 (18 March 1960), pp. 1,5.

Jefferson, Thomas. *The Papers of Thomas Jefferson.* Ed. Julian P. Boyd. 17 vols. Princeton: Princeton University Press, 1951–.

————————. *The Writings of Thomas Jefferson.* Ed. A. A. Lipscomb and A. E. Bergh. 20 vols. Washington: Thomas Jefferson Memorial Association, 1903-1904.

John Norton & Sons, Merchants of London and Virginia. Ed. Frances Norton Mason. Richmond: Dietz Press, 1937.

Johnson, Charles. *The Country Lasses: or the Custom of the Manor.* London, 1753.

"Journal of a French Traveller in the Colonies, 1765," *American Historical Review*, XXVI (1920-1921), No. 4, 726-747.

Krutch, Joseph Wood. *Comedy and Conscience after the Restoration.* New York: Columbia University Press, 1961.

Lee, Henry. *Memoirs of the War in the Southern Department.* Revised and edited by Robert E. Lee. New York: University Publishing Co., 1870.

Lewis, George E. *The Indiana Company, 1763-1798.* Glendale, Calif.: Arthur H. Clark Co., 1941.

The Literature of the South. Ed. Richmond Croom Beatty, Floyd C. Watkins, and Thomas Daniel Young. Chicago: Scott. Foresman, and Co., 1952.

Lunenburg County. *Sunlight on the Southside.* Ed. Landon C. Bell. Philadelphia: George S. Ferguson Co., 1931.

McAllister, J. T., ed. *Virginia Militia in the Revolutionary War.* Hot Springs, Va.: McAllister Publishing Co., 1913.

McCrady, Edward. *The History of South Carolina in the Revolution, 1775-1780.* New York: Macmillan, 1902.

McCullough, Rose Chambers Goode. *Yesterday When it is Past.* Richmond: William Byrd Press, 1957.

McGhee, Lucy Kate. *Virginia Pension Abstracts of the Wars of the Revolution, 1812 and Indian Wars.* 17 vols. Washington: privately printed, 1959–.

McGill, John, compiler. *The Beverley Family of Virginia.* Columbia, S. C.: R. L. Bryan Co., 1956.

McIlwaine, H. R., ed. "Justices of the Peace of Colonial Virginia," Virginia State Library *Bulletin*, XIV (April, July, 1921), 37-149.

Malone, Dumas. *Jefferson the Virginian.* Boston: Little, Brown, and Co., 1948.

Manly, Louise. *Southern Literature from 1579 to 1895.* Richmond: B. F. Johnson Publishing Co., 1895.

Mays, David John. *Edmund Pendleton, 1721-1803.* 2 vols. Cambridge:

Harvard University Press, 1952.

Meade, Robert Douthat. *Patrick Henry, Patriot in the Making.* Philadelphia: Lippincott, 1957.

Meade, William. *Old Churches, Ministers, and Families of Virginia.* 2 vols. Philadelphia: Lippincott, 1906.

Mecklenburg County. *Early Settlers, Mecklenburg County, Virginia.* Compiled by Katherine B. Elliott. 2 vols. South Hill, Va.: Mrs. Elliott, 1964 and 1965.

———. *Early Wills, 1765-1799, Mecklenburg County, Virginia.* Compiled by Mrs. Katherine B. Elliott. South Hill, Va.: Mrs. Elliott, 1963.

———. *The Marriage License Bonds of Mecklenburg County, Virginia, from 1765 to 1810.* Abstracted by John T. Hutcheson and listed by Stratton Nottingham. Onancock, Va.: privately printed, 1928.

———. *Marriage Records—1765-1810, Mecklenburg County, Virginia.* Compiled by Katherine B. Elliott. South Hill, Va.: Mrs. Elliott, 1963.

———. *Revolutionary War Records, Mecklenburg County, Virginia.* Compiled by Mrs. Katherine B. Elliott. South Hill, Va.: Mrs. Elliott, 1964.

Norton, Richard L. *Colonial Virginia.* 2 vols. Chapel Hill: University of North Carolina Press for the Virginia Historical Society, 1960.

Moses, Montrose J. *The American Dramatist,* Boston: Little, Brown, and Co., 1925.

———. *Literature of the South.* New York: T. Y. Crowell and Co., 1910.

Munford, Beverley B. *Random Recollections.* New York: De Vinne Press, 1905.

Munford, Robert. *A Collection of Plays and Poems, by the late Colonel Robert Munford, of Mecklenburg, in the State of Virginia.* Petersburg, 1798. Readings throughout are based on the Readex microprint of the copy in the American Antiquarian Society Library.

Munford, William. *Poems and Compositions in Prose on Several Occasions.* Richmond, 1798.

North Carolina. *North Carolina Colonial Records* and *State Records.* Ed. William L. Saunders and Walter Clark. 26 vols. Raleigh, Goldsboro, and Winston, N. C., 1886-1907.

Peacock, Matthew Henry. *History of the Free Grammar School at Wakefield.* Wakefield: W. H. Milnes, 1892.

Philadelphia. Library Company of Philadelphia. *A Catalogue of the Books Belonging to the Library Company of Philadelphia.* 2 vols. Philadelphia: C. Sherman and Co., 1835.

Princess Anne County. *Marriages of Princess Anne County, 1749-1821.* Compiled by Elizabeth B. Wingo. n.p.: privately printed, 1961.

Quinn, Arthur Hobson. *A History of the American Drama from the Beginning to the Civil War.* New York: Harper and Brothers, 1923. Also 2nd. ed. New York: Appleton-Century-Crofts, 1951.

Rankin, Hugh F. *The Theater in Colonial America.* Chapel Hill: University of North Carolina Press, 1960, 1965.

Rowland, Kate Mason. *The Life of George Mason.* 2 vols. New York: G. P. Putnam's, 1892.

Sabin, Joseph. *Bibliotheca Americana.* 29 vols. New York: Bibliographical Society of America, 1868-1936.

Sabine, Lorenzo. *Biographical Sketches of Loyalists of the American Revolution.* 2 vols. Boston: Little, Brown, 1864.

Salley, A. S., Jr. "Capt. John Colcock and Some of his Descendants," *The South Carolina Historical and Genealogical Magazine,* III (October, 1902), 219-220.

Seilhamer, George O. *History of the American Theatre.* 3 vols. Philadelphia: Globe Printing House, 1888-1891.

Semple. Robert B. *A History of the Rise and Progress of the Baptists in Virginia.* Revised and extended by G. W. Beale. Richmond: Pitt and Dickerson, 1894.

Slaughter, Philip. *A History of Bristol Parish, Virginia.* 2nd. ed. Richmond: J. W. Randolph and English, 1879.

Smith, John. *The General Historie of Virginia, New England & the Summer Isles.* 2 vols. Glasgow: J. Mac Lehose and Sons, 1907.

Speed, Thomas. *Records and Memorials of the Speed Family.* Louisville: Courier-Journal Co., 1892.

Taylor, James B. *Lives of Virginia Baptist Ministers.* 2nd. ed. Richmond: Yale and Wyatt, 1838.

Tucker, Nathaniel Beverley. Review of William Munford's translation of Homer's *Iliad. Southern Literary Messenger,* XII (July, 1846), 445-452.

Tyler, Lyon Gardiner. *Williamsburg, the Old Colonial Capital.* Richmond: Whittet and Shepperson, 1907.

Tyler's Quarterly Historical and Genealogical Magazine.

United States, Department of Commerce and Labor, Bureau of the Census. *Heads of Families . . . 1790; Records of State Enumerations: 1782 to 1785.* Washington, 1908.

Virginia. *Calendar of Virginia State Papers.* Ed. H. W. Flournoy, William P. Palmer, et al. 11 vols. Richmond, 1875-1893. Cited as CSP.

Virginia, Council of State. *Journals of the Council of the State of Virginia.* Ed. H. R. McIlwaine. 3 vols. Richmond, 1931-1932.

Virginia, General Assembly. *The Statutes at Large; Being a Collection of All the Laws of Virginia.* Ed. by William Walter Hening. 13 vols. Richmond, 1809-1823. Cited as Hening.

Virginia, House of Burgesses. *Journals of the House of Burgesses.* Ed. John P. Kennedy and H. R. McIlwaine. 13 vols. Richmond, 1905-1915. Cited as *JHB.*

Virginia, House of Delegates. *Journals of the House of Delegates of Virginia.* . . . [for sessions 1779-1786] 4 vols. Richmond, 1827-28. Cited as *JHD.*

Virginia, Supreme Court of Appeals. *Reports of Cases Argued and Determined in the Court of Appeals of Virginia.* Reported by Bushrod Washington, *et al.* 18 vols. Richmond, 1798-1819.

The Virginia Gazette.

The Virginia Gazette, or the American Advertiser.

The Virginia Historical Register.

The Virginia Magazine of History and Biography.

Washington, George. *The Writings of George Washington.* Ed. John C. Fitzpatrick. 39 vols. Washington: Government Printing Office, 1931-1944.

Wegelin, Oscar. *Early American Plays, 1714-1830.* New York: Dunlap Society, 1900. Also 2nd. ed. New York: Literary Collector Press, 1905.

――――――. *Early American Poetry.* 2nd. ed. New York: P. Smith, 1930.

The William and Mary Quarterly.

Wyatt, Edward Avery, IV. *Along Petersburg Streets.* Richmond: Dietz Press, 1943.

Wyatt, Edward Avery, IV, ed. *Preliminary Checklist for Petersburg. Virginia Imprint Series,* No. 9. Richmond: Virginia State Library, 1949.

Index

Robert Munford

America's First Comic Dramatist
BY RODNEY M. BAINE

Robert Munford of Virginia wrote America's first dramatic farce and first legitimate comedy in the late 1700's. For more than a century his work remained virtually unknown and inaccessible. Only within the last few decades have his plays been reprinted.

In this biography Dr. Baine supplies previously unavailable information of Munford's early life and his career as a Virginia Burgess, military officer, and gentleman-planter. He also corrects some erroneous facts about Munford's life: for example, his birth (1737) has always been moved ahead to "before 1730".

The last part of the book is devoted to a critical study of Munford's plays, *The Candidates* and *The Patriots*. The author provides a local milieu for the appreciation of characterization and allusion in the plays and analyzes them in the light of English comedy popular in colonial Virginia.

UNIVERSITY OF GEORGIA PRESS
ATHENS